New Library of Pastoral Care
GENERAL EDITOR: DEREK BLOWS

Derek Blows is the Director of the Westminster Pastoral
Foundation, a psychotherapist at University College
Hospital, and a Professional Member of the Society of
Analytical Psychology. He is also an honorary canon of
Southwark Cathedral.

KT-475-970

Clergy Stress

£4/4

Titles in this series include:

New Library of Pastoral Care
GENERAL EDITOR: DEREK BLOWS

———

CLERGY STRESS

The Hidden Conflicts in Ministry

———

Mary Anne Coate

First published in Great Britain 1989
SPCK
Holy Trinity Church
Marylebone Road
London NW1 4DU

Third impression 1990

British Library Cataloguing in Publication Data

Coate, Mary Anne
  Clergy stress
  1. Christian church. Clergy. Stress
  I. Title   II. Series
  253'.2
  ISBN 0-281-04409-0

Filmset by Pioneer
Printed and bound in Great Britain by
Courier International Ltd, Tiptree, Essex

Contents

Foreword

The New Library of Pastoral Care has been planned to meet
the needs of those people concerned with pastoral care,
whether clergy or lay, who seek to improve their knowledge
and skills in this field. Equally, it is hoped that it may prove
useful to those secular helpers who may wish to understand
the role of the pastor.

Pastoral care in every age has drawn from contemporary
secular knowledge to inform its understanding of man and
his various needs and of the ways in which these needs might
be met. Today it is perhaps the secular helping professions of
social work, counselling and psychotherapy, and community
development which have particular contributions to make to
the pastor in his work. Such knowledge does not stand still,
and a pastor would have a struggle to keep up with the
endless tide of new developments which pour out from these
and other disciplines, and to sort out which ideas and
practices might be relevant to his particular pastoral needs.
Among present-day ideas, for instance, of particular value
might be an understanding of the social context of the pastoral
task, the dynamics of the helping relationship, the attitudes
and skills as well as factual knowledge which might make for
effective pastoral intervention and, perhaps most significant
of all, the study of particular cases, whether through verbatim
reports of interviews or general case presentation. The
discovery of ways of learning from what one is doing is
becoming increasingly important.

There is always a danger that a pastor who drinks deeply
at the well of a secular discipline may lose his grasp of his
own pastoral identity and become 'just another' social worker
or counsellor. It in no way detracts from the value of these
professions to assert that the role and task of the pastor are
quite unique among the helping professions and deserve to be

clarified and strengthened rather than weakened. The theological commitment of the pastor and the appropriate use of his role will be a recurrent theme of the series. At the same time the pastor cannot afford to work in a vacuum. He needs to be able to communicate and co-operate with those helpers in other disciplines whose work may overlap, without loss of his own unique role. This in turn will mean being able to communicate with them through some understanding of their concepts and language.

Finally, there is a rich variety of styles and approaches in pastoral work within the various religious traditions. No attempt will be made to secure a uniform approach. The Library will contain the variety, and even perhaps occasional eccentricity, which such a title suggests. Some books will be more specifically theological and others more concerned with particular areas of need or practice. It is hoped that all of them will have a usefulness that will reach right across the boundaries of religious denomination.

DEREK BLOWS
Series Editor

Acknowledgements

The pages that follow were born of my reflections over many years, and so represent the working over of diverse experiences with contributions coming from many sources. What I have taken in has become what I can only describe as a 'Christmas pudding' mixture, stirred many times, and it is difficult now to identify and acknowledge the original ingredients.

When I was compiling the chapter references and footnotes I found my memory often playing me false; a name wrong here, two or three years out there or a quotation slightly misworded, no doubt to suit the sense I wanted to see and remember in it . . . I have tried, as far as I can, to acknowledge my written sources and to do so correctly, but need here to apologize for such omissions and errors as may remain.

As with written sources, so with my immeasurable debt to people. I cannot now disentangle the exact and individual contributions of all those with whom I have lived and worked over the years in settings within and outside ministry. Nevertheless I want to voice here my gratitude for all I have been given. At this present moment of finishing writing I should like to thank, first, Judith Longman of SPCK and Derek Blows, the series editor, for their encouragement to persevere, their willingness to enter into dialogue with my thinking and their patient wrestling with the style of my writing (such convolutions as are left are those I have inexorably managed to slip in), and second, my friends who have generously and with forbearing put up with my being rather engrossed and sometimes of a one-track mind.

Finally, I should like to say that my reflection, though the most thorough-going I can make up to this point, is not final.

It is and always has been ever-changing. For this I make no apology — for I have a fundamental belief that our search for truth is unending and is constantly refreshed by new experience and deeper questions — except in so far as my 'unfinishedness' makes my readers struggle overmuch in the dialogue between their stories and mine.

Mary Anne Coate
February 1989

Introduction

Inevitably, I have been asking myself why I should have wanted to write a book of this nature, and my preliminary answer can only be that is has been germinating over a period of years and is now asking to be written.

Yet the act of writing is a sort of 'giving birth', and as such arouses anxiety as to whether the 'infant' will be at all like its cherished internal image. Here the answer, again inevitably I suppose, seems to be that to some degree it will not and cannot. For in the process of externalization ideas and feelings must be put into words; this gives them organization and some necessary boundaries, but something also is lost. Something of free flowingness — of interconnection at intangible levels — is interrupted when ideas-become-words hit the light of day. The sense of unity that seems real when it is inside me has to meet the outside world, which may break it up, take bits — and indeed leave bits — in ways I had never envisaged. It may even be that the whole conception cannot withstand the ravages of birth. But that is a risk I have to take.

My avowed aim is to write, as far as possible without using technical 'jargon', in the difficult overlap area between the disciplines of theology and psychology. This overlap is, I believe, vital to the well-being and development of the Church and other religious bodies, and indeed to religious faith itself. I am, though, aware that this belief may not be self-evident to others and may require justification, which I hope to attempt. At some points I shall find myself unable to name, exactly, my source just because it has become a part of me and my experience. Other points will perhaps link up with the experience and thought of others and the past in ways that are more directly and immediately recognizable. The essential nature of such an enterprise is that it is and indeed must be

1

tentative. In one sense nothing can be proved, and the viability of the enterprise will to a large extent stand or fall in its interplay and interaction with the world into which it comes.

Much of what I want to say comes from my reflection upon twenty years of life in the Church of England, first as a member of a religious community and then as part of a diocesan team. But it is also the product of several years' discussion in two groups, one a support group for people from different caring professions and with different religious affiliations, and the other focusing more specifically on the exploration of Jewish Christian relationships. So, intimate reflection on the religious life and on the task of ministry from inside it has helped to mould and inform the more personal 'me', as has my experience of personal therapy, which, above all, has facilitated me to begin to look beneath the surface with, I hope, a healthy curiosity towards the question 'What quite is going on?'. This question is of course particularly relevant when we sense that our internal growth and well-being are being frustrated by ourselves. The issue then becomes that of beginning to see that in the confusion of our inner thoughts and feelings and, quite possibly, its consequences, in distorted relationships with the outside world, there lies also the potential for integration and growth.

I am needing, however, to reflect not only upon my personal experience, but also upon that of actual work orientated towards other people and external reality. I owe much both to my previous posts within the Church, working with clergy, Religious and lay people in the areas of theological reflection, human relations and counselling, and to my more recent work in the National Health Service. Although this last did not necessarily involve the 'religious' dimension of life it has helped me to bring together the other experiences and to begin to try to integrate them into some sort of whole. I draw also upon my continued experience as a member of the English Association for Pastoral Care and Counselling and its associated movement in Europe.[1] Conferences, in particular, mounted by these groups have offered time and space for engagement with such themes as freedom, mature and immature religion, conflict and pain, and power in pastoral care.

I have never accepted a dichotomy between inwardly

orientated individual exploration and that undertaken by or on behalf of the wider community. I have always felt that there is a constant interplay between them, and that increased understanding of ourselves acts both as the foundation point, and as one constant source of illumination, of the process of trying to understand the communities and the world of which we are a part. Indeed this belief is part of the thesis of this book. The extent to which it is realistic and is being realized will, I hope, be clarified through what follows.

What I am not intending to write about

I am not going to write about sociology or structures, nor will I describe in detail the various schemes that have been proposed or are already in use to facilitate changes in the system. This is done more fully elsewhere in the various reports and books on ministry that are already available. I am not wanting in any way to denigrate the work in this field, nor is it the focus of what I want to say. I will rather take these explorations and experiments for granted and allude to them as appropriate. Neither am I wanting to write primarily about the management of stress and anxiety through the use of relaxation and similar coping techniques. Again, these are important and form part of a wider literature dealing with the effect of stress in all our lives, and I have included a short account of them in Chapter 10,[2] together with some pointers towards further resources. Perhaps here I should comment on my use of the word 'stress'. This has many connotations ranging from every discomfort in the face of pressure to a more technical usage in physiological and psychological literature. I am going to take it to refer either to the discomfort felt by a person or group whilst under pressure, which may show itself in physiological, emotional or even action (behavioural) ways, or to the source of the pressure itself. In psychological literature[3] this latter is more properly differentiated from stress and referred to as the 'stressor', but I prefer to retain the widest meaning of the word stress, even at the cost of some loss in precise thinking.

It may be that the reader is going to feel cheated if he or she comes to read these pages primarily hoping for and expecting concrete and practical help in the *management* of anxieties and even symptoms. If this is so, I will need to admit the charge, not because I think that getting this help is unimportant, but because the knowledge concerning it is available elsewhere. Whereas, at least to my knowledge, not so much work has hitherto gone into trying to understand the *causes of* and *more hidden factors in* these unpleasant experiences as they obtrude into the life and ministry of church or synagogue.

What I do intend to write about

I want to attempt to reflect on ministry from *inside* the religious dimension: 'inside' in the sense of trying to understand what may be going on within ministers and between them and their congregation, clients, neighbours and colleagues. This is not all, for there is another level which defies articulation. I am talking of a sort of climate of the whole religious tradition which encompasses both ministers and congregation. 'Climate' is not quite the right word but I feel it best expresses the sense of something amorphous, not easily observable, which transcends both individuals and even the corporate bodies as these are constituted at any one point in time.

From this the reader will ascertain that I am wanting to emphasize the feelings and fantasies that we do not easily observe precisely because we are part of them and they emanate from a part of our being of which we are not easily aware. Moreover, we put some considerable energy into not becoming aware of them because they might arouse questioning and anxiety beyond that which we can comfortably tolerate. This is not because we are necessarily moral or emotional cowards; to suggest this is a mistake sometimes made by enthusiasts who feel that everyone should face everything all the time without any defences. It seems to me that since religion does attempt to be open to the depths and ultimate questions of life which are inevitably threatening as well as exhilarating, it is impossible to be equally open to them all the time.

I am, however, committed to the belief that greater exploring and understanding, at a pace that we can tolerate, does ultimately help to contain and relieve anxiety. I want, therefore, to push back the frontiers of such exploration in this book, at least to some extent. Yet because we thereby enter the realm of what is not easily testable or provable it is important that this exploration should be seen for what it is — tentative and leaving space for disagreement and modification as well as for further exploration. I have in mind three active ingredients:

(1) I would like to try to tell a story to see if it is recognizable as part of *the* story that none of us can tell in its entirety since none of us can know all the characters, talk all the languages or understand all the levels of meaning.

I wish to emphasize this point since there is the ever-present danger for most of us of claiming the name of absolute truth for our latest approximation to it. We perhaps think that we can answer Pilate's original question 'What is Truth?';[4] indeed some will claim that it is already definitively answered for us in the Christian tradition, but I am suggesting that in its essence and totality it remains as unanswerable now as it was to Pilate 2,000 years ago.

(2) I am *attempting* to bring together theological and psychological insights, which in itself is a tall order! I am not thinking in terms of a technical treatise from the viewpoint of either discipline, and am likely therefore to offend the purists of both, for it is my conviction that any attempt at bridging the gap between disciplines inevitably involves a loss of tidiness and purity, though this is not intended as a 'cop-out' apology in advance for sloppy thinking. Indeed, in the post-script which follows Chapter 6, I want to offer an under-standing of one of the central themes of Christianity, namely redemption and atonement, in a way that I hope will do justice both to theology and psychology. I want to attempt this partly to illustrate a point that is central to an inter-disciplinary enterprise. We cannot know or trust in advance that theological and psychological insights will always be amenable to each other; or, alternatively, that they will always be in sharp conflict with each other, as has sometimes been feared. My hope is that the psychological dimension may help to give our theology depth, and what I can only call an 'internal' meaning for us. But in this process it may well be

that moments of illumination are interspersed with points of sharp conflict, and that not all these latter will be resolvable.

One of the difficulties in this area has been that the revolution in psychological thinking came about through the work and writing of Freud, and his views on religion have often been quoted out of the context both of the time in which he was writing and of developments in his own thinking. The parody of Freud that has tended to pass into popular thought runs something like this: 'He was only interested in sex, and regarded religion as the subjective expression of the purely human longing for a strong parent.' This parody, besides being grossly unfair to the breadth and depth of his thought and development, has effectively insulated theological thinking from having to take seriously the challenge he could pose as part of the task of discriminating mature and immature elements in religious faith. With a few notable exceptions,[5] the dialogue between religious belief and modern psychology has been resisted.

It does seem that the thought of Jung has been more acceptable than that of Freud since there have been more attempts to interpret his work in the light of religious thinking.[6] It may be that people have thought that there is less conflict here, that Jung is more naturally amenable to agreement with faith. For myself I am not so sure that this is self-evident, though such a discussion would need another book. Suffice it to say here that it is my impression, overall, that the *content* of theology has not been allowed very much encounter with psychology.

Two 'half-way' stages *have* been defined. The first consists in drawing upon some of the insights of the psychological, and particularly the psychotherapeutic, dimension in the service of *applied* theology, namely pastoral care and counselling.[7] The second uses a developmental model of how human beings gradually acquire the ability to symbolize in order to explain the process through which religious belief and faith are made possible.[8]

These half-way stages have had the effect of allowing the theological story to retain its privileged place in relation to the *content* of belief about God and ultimate reality, whilst allowing to psychological thinking a limited place in illuminating the *way* in which this belief relates to actual human living. But in this insight is obscured a fundamental point, namely that the content and process of theological reflection is not 'pure' and does not come out of a vacuum. It has always made use of some other level of thinking. The exegesis of, for example, the Gospel of St John and the Epistle to the Colossians has turned on the question as to whether Hebrew thought or Greek philosophy or even a mixture of the two[9] should be seen as underlying them. Similarly, the theological thinking of the early Church Fathers made use of either a Greek or Latin heritage and an underlying Platonic or Aristotelian philosophy, and theology came out differently according to variations in this underlying base.[10]

Theological reflection has also inevitably depended on human experience, both corporate and personal. For example, St Anselm's doctrine of the atonement in terms of debts owed and satisfaction being made[11] makes sense in terms of his experience of the feudal system of his day, whereas Abelard's alternative theory perhaps owes much to his personal experience of human love through his relationship with Heloise.[12] Equally, St Paul and St Augustine have different theological interpretations of the undoubted fact of man failing to realize the potential of his highest values. St Paul in Romans 7[13] implies it is due to his inability, and St Augustine to an exercise of free will.[14] These, it seems to me, must come out of differing human experiences creating differing views on human psychology.

So theology contains an implicit psychology, and whilst this remains only implicit and is not acknowledged and made explicit, dialogue cannot take place. Much potentially fruitful reflection and development are therefore lost; much potential for conflict is also lost. Indeed this may be the point, that people somehow fear that that conflict would, necessarily, be destructive of faith and they thus avoid it.

Nevertheless, the contribution to theology of reflection on human experience has always been there, even if not acknowledged. What the advent of modern psychology has done is to extend this beyond the realm of the rational so as to include elements from our less rational and unconscious selves. If we can use it, the picture can be richer and more complete even if it inevitably also introduces elements of uncertainty and confusion.

(3) Throughout what follows I am seeing clergy and ministers as members of one of the caring professions, and so subject to the pressures of all such jobs. But ministry is also unique with particular pressures stemming from the specifically religious dimension, and from vocation to service within it. So there will be sources of stress for ministers that are not shared by other caring professionals. Moreover they are likely to be permanent and insidious and so may go unrecognized and unalleviated unless and until they force themselves on our attention in threatening and potentially destructive ways.

Among the most likely effects of stress are illness — either life-threatening or chronically debilitating, dependence on alcohol or other drugs, personal emotional breakdown, marital breakdown in those religious traditions in which marriage is allowed and difficulties with celibacy in those where it is not. There may also be an external move out of ministry or a more internal move away from any sense of vocation. More ubiquitous and far more difficult to detect is a sort of adjustment which looks all right on the surface, but which actually is inhibiting the fulfilment of our potential, both for our task of ministry and for our development as human beings.

Alleviation of strain will depend on trying to understand its causes as fully as we can; otherwise we shall bypass the real problem and the stress and strain are likely to build up again when the impact and impetus of first-aid measures have faded.

Finally, I need to say that, whilst I am well aware of the debate that centres on the use or non-use of 'inclusive' language in religious and church matters, I am *not* scrupulously following it in my writing. I shall, when talking both of God and human beings, use either masculine or feminine nouns and pronouns according to which seem appropriate to the style and flow of the sentence in which they have to appear. This is for two reasons. First, I feel that to attempt to write continuously and consciously in inclusive language is actually cumbersome and inimical to the free flow of writing and so, ultimately, to communication. Second, it is precisely because the debate is important that I do not want to pre-empt it by apparently coming down on one side of it. I am concerned, rather, that we should try to *understand* both why the issue has become important and what underlies it. From this viewpoint it forms part of the content, not the presentation, of my reflection.

Notes

1. Established 1970: subsequently a founder member, then a division, of The British Association for Counselling.
2. See Chapter 10; pp. 198—201.
3. For an account of the definition and nature of stress see T. Cox *Stress,* Macmillan 1978.
4. John 18.38.
5. See, for example: E. Fromm *Psychoanalysis and Religion,* Yale University Press 1950; Heiji Faber *The Psychology of Religion,* SCM 1976; or the work of Joachim Scharfenberg of the Institute of Practical Theology, Kiel, West Germany.
6. See, for example: Victor White OP *God and the Unconscious,* Harvill Press 1952; Christopher Bryant *Depth Psychology and Religious Belief,* Mirfield Publications 1972.
7. Now a European and international movement with established training programmes (e.g. Clinical Pastoral Training in the USA) for relating theological and psychological insights in the practice of ministry. See also, in the UK, departments of pastoral studies in universities and theological colleges, and diocesan initiatives in Pastoral Care and Counselling.
8. See, for example, J. W. Fowler *Stages of Faith,* San Fransisco, Harper and Row 1981.
9. See commentaries: C. H. Dodd *Interpretation of the Fourth Gospel,* Cambridge University Press 1953; C. F. D. Moule *Epistle of Paul the Apostle to the Colossians and Philemon,* Cambridge Greek Testament commentary 1957.
10. See chs. 5 and 6 of G. L. Prestige *Fathers and Heretics,* SPCK 1940.
11. St Anselm *Cur Deus Homo;* see J. M. Rigg *S. Anselm,* London 1896.
12. See Peter Abelard, Letters to Heloise, 5, in Betty Radice, *Letters of Abelard and Heloise,* Penguin 1974.
13. Romans 7.19.
14. St Augustine of Hippo *On Rebuke and Grace,* 33.

ONE

Introducing People

I would like to start by inviting you to consider some imaginary snippets of conversation. Their subject is the minister's *day off*. A tiny area, we could think, but I suggest symptomatic of the whole.

A minister may say: 'Yes, I know it's my day off, but I just thought I should visit *this* family in such particular need, deal with the diocesan returns which after all need an uninterrupted period of time, or attend this special meeting of the PCC which couldn't be put on any other day, could it?'

Or a member of the congregation may say: 'Yes, I know it's really your day off, but this really won't wait and I did just notice from your car being there that you hadn't gone out today.' Or: 'I'm sorry to bother you at a meal time, on a Monday too, but I knew it would be the only time I could be sure of getting you.' Or, most insidiously: 'I know you wouldn't want *most* people calling in on your day off, but I thought you wouldn't mind *me* just this once as I suddenly realized that if only I could talk over this worrying question today everything would be so much better and clearer.'

Given the advent of modern technology we not infrequently have: 'I suppose you do have to have an answer-phone, but it does mean that the personal touch is gone.'

Herein lie the seeds of conflict. Recommendations have been made to the effect that ministers should be left free from intrusion on one day in the week. Yet somehow these do not seem to work very well in practice. The difficulty is compounded because of the sneaking thought, often bitten back, among non-ministers that the minister only *really* works on Sunday!

We could multiply these sorts of conversations and adapt them to issues other than days off. We can see immediately that often it is not the work of one party only. A minister may find it difficult or impossible to resist demands, especially when they are couched in such a way as to imply that the principles of pastoral care are at stake. Congregations may, for their part, find it difficult or impossible not to make demands, especially if in other ways they see their minister very much as the leader or 'father' of the parish or religious community. If challenged, however, both parties would, in all probability, insist that they were respecting the spirit if not the letter of the law. When confronted by actual evidence the most likely response is, 'Well, that was an exception.'

The problem of strain and stress in ministry is encapsulated in the mismatch of human need and demand and the capacity to give. The example above comes from the present time, but the story has a history: the life of St Paul stands as one of the first and greatest examples of Christian ministry. But we see from his letters that strain and turmoil among those charged to proclaim the gospel and to care for others who are similarly involved are not an invention of the twentieth century. Consider this passage:

> Three times I have been beaten with rods; once I was stoned. Three times I have been shipwrecked; a night and a day I have been adrift at sea; on frequent journeys, in danger from robbers, danger from my own people, danger from Gentiles, danger in the city, danger in the wilderness, danger at sea, danger from false brethren; in toil and hardship, through many a sleepless night, in hunger and thirst, often without food, in cold and exposure. And, apart from other things, there is the daily pressure upon me of my anxiety for all the churches.[1]

Few present-day ministers — at least in Britain — are required to go through such trials and dangers to personal safety and survival as was St Paul. But it is not so foreign to our experience to talk of 'the daily pressures of anxiety'. — Or is it? Immediately there may be some who will contest this, maintaining that the work of ministry is a fulfilling joy, and that anxiety and disturbance among ministers betray a lack of trust in the fundamental faith and truth of the gospel. Such people would probably want to counter Corinthians with St John: 'Let not your hearts be troubled; believe in God, believe also in me.'[2] Or St Luke:

. . .do not be anxious about your life . . . which of you by
being anxious can add a cubit to his span of life? If then
you are not able to do as small a thing as that, why are you
anxious about the rest? . . . Fear not, little flock, for it is
your Father's good pleasure to give you the kingdom.[3]

There are also likely to be those who say something like
this: 'Clergy and ministers are free from a lot of the strains
and worries that beset other people. They have tenure in their
job, the security of a home, and the continued support of a
caring hierarchy. If perhaps their earnings are less than
average for those of similar age and with comparable training
and experience, then that pertains to the nature of vocation,
and is only right and to be expected.'

Every so often correspondence and articles in church and
other newspapers make a suggestion of hardship and stress
among the clergy; in recent years the plight of deserted clergy
wives, the difficulties of managing a family on a lowish
income and the problem of job-finding have all been
highlighted.[4] The ensuing debate is nearly always double-
edged: for every reader in sympathy, there will nearly always
be another making the point that the ways of the Church (or
Synagogue) as an employer do not conform to the ways of the
secular world, and should not be expected to do so.

So strain among clergy and ministers of religion seems in
some ways not to be quite 'respectable'. Indeed it is often
denied, and it is partly this tendency to denial that constrained
me to try to write about it. For my conviction is that strain
and disturbance, sometimes very acute and painful and
sometimes more insidious and chronic, *do* exist and need
bringing into the light and to be understood. First because
they cause too much human suffering that could be alleviated,
and second because they result in ministers, and indeed the
Church itself, often functioning way below their true
potential.

It is not of course the case that nothing has been recognized.
The Diocese of Bath and Wells has published a report on just
this subject of stress in ministers.[5] In 1985 it was revealed
that up to 40 per cent of clergy marriages are thought to be,
at one time or another, in serious difficulty.[6] Over the last
twenty years there has been a very large exodus of Religious,

both Anglican and Catholic, from their orders and their vows. And there are the occasional scandals of greater magnitude involving clergymen which, irresistibly it seems, make the national news.

These are the more obvious and overt signs that all is not well. Less obvious are the incidences of illness, both major and minor, among the clergy, and the fact of a not inconsiderable number of clergy feeling the need to depart from the Church's ministry and go into secular employment. More insidious still is the sense of being stuck in a rut, with a draining of creativity and/or a retreat into a sense of isolation or simply mountains of paper work.

It is not only ministers themselves who are affected. If married, their families suffer from the apparent security of the 'tied' home which carries within it the sense that nowhere quite is 'home'. Many clergy try to offset this sense of underlying insecurity by saving for a 'cottage in the country' which at least is theirs, independently of whatever 'home' is provided by the job. But the low level of clergy salaries often makes this an impossibility. Many people in this country know the pain and difficulty of not owning their own home; what is not so easily recognized is that the clergy share this pain. This is but one of the more hidden sources of stress in what appears on the surface to be a rather secure existence.

In addition, many clergy wives now work. They maintain that they have to in order to maintain a reasonable standard of living, and in any case many of them want a career of their own and not to be merely the extension of their husband's ministry. On a practical level this can make for increased difficulty in keeping going any sort of family life, for husband and wife are likely to have different timetables. On a deeper level conflicts arise over the competing claims of 'mere jobs' and 'overriding vocations'.

Other pressures come from the inevitable changes that have taken place in the task of ministry over the years. I think that most people would be able to agree that we are a far cry from the pattern of ministry advocated and practised by such as George Reindorp.[7] In the days of which he was writing a minister could reasonably expect to pray or study in the mornings, visit his (for it was *he* in those days) parish or patch in the afternoons, and probably attend meetings or other functions in the evenings. This pattern no longer fits easily with that of the rest of the working world, nor the availability of the people with whom the minister needs to be in contact. This problem is probably seen most clearly in urban and inner-city areas, but is not absent from more rural settings.

There are other difficulties, those inherent in the work of ministry itself. What exactly are we supposed to be trained to do? Is our rightful sphere confined to the task of preaching the gospel to such as want to hear it, and to evangelizing those who do not, or are we to operate in a wider role within our parish and our general socio-cultural setting? Our sense of ambiguity is often complicated by the reaction of those in the world around us. Bocock, in a study undertaken in 1970,[8] suggested that the secular world had come to evaluate ministry solely as one of the 'helping professions' akin to the social services. The result of this for ourselves as ministers is that we can feel inadequate because of our lack of a recognized professional training and qualification in this new area. Operating in a wider sphere than that envisaged by much theological training, at least that of the past, apparently calls for skills in administration, management, counselling and social and political awareness. It is therefore necessary for us to try to 'pick up' these skills, by, for example, going on counselling or management courses, whilst at the same time feeling resentful that we were not better prepared in our initial training. Sometimes we embrace the new discipline so single-mindedly that the original purpose of ministry gets crowded out; we become 'counsellors' — to take one possibility — and do not want to do *just* 'pastoral care'.[9]

It is of course possible to reject such an 'extended' role for ministers, and indeed some of the outcry against the Church's current 'interference' in politics would suggest that some people prefer to see the Church operating only in its 'own' sphere and 'own' place. But for those of us who do feel that in all conscience our task is to encompass the concerns and issues of the wider community, the questions that face us are likely to be manifold, and the sense of confusion and inadequacy sometimes paralysing.

It is important not to underestimate or devalue what has been done to mitigate strain and stress. Many dioceses now put considerable emphasis on in-service training, recognizing that continuing input is needed to overcome problems of fatigue and staleness. There has been growing attention to the issue of job satisfaction, and to the reverse side of that coin, accountability, with a number of dioceses setting up schemes for the continuing review of a minister's life and work. However, such schemes are sometimes perceived as containing a hidden threat in much the same way as the thought of any sort of evaluation is perceived. Though its aim is to support and encourage us to make better use of gifts and achievements whilst learning from such mistakes as must happen, our instinctive reaction tends to be that we shall be weighed in the balance and found wanting!

On the more personal level there is now much more emphasis on adequate time off, opportunities for recreation and even the possibility of sabbaticals and time away from the 'patch'. Some dioceses have set up schemes whereby ministers can meet in groups to share and discuss both insights and problems.[10] It has also been possible to provide a time and space for bishops and more senior Church leaders to meet and look at their particular issues in comparative privacy.[11] It would, therefore, be grossly unfair to say that nothing is being or has been done.

It is not uncommon, however, to find that only a minority of ministers find themselves able to take advantage of such changes. Yet we can get 'lulled' into trusting that, because reports on such themes as stress and the state of clergy marriages have been written and recommendations made, the situation will thereby almost automatically get better.

I want to emphasize here that I am *not* doubting the sincerity of all concerned. I see it much more as an example of St Paul's dictum, 'the good things I would I do not, and the evil I would not, that I do'.[12] I want to take time, in these chapters, to try to explore a little of why, with the best intentions in the world, our efforts towards the relief of strain sometimes seem to come to nothing.

I think it is partly, and quite powerfully, because for a lot of our time we think and act from the level of our *conscious* awareness, and cannot be aware of more hidden pressures that can be very strong and militate against change. This has to do with strong stereotypes and also with our personal histories, that sometimes seem to impel us to get entangled in these stereotypes. To take an example: it is possible for ministers in general and any of us in particular to have a powerful picture/stereotype of ourselves as always pastorally available for the care of the flock whenever they may seem to need it. We may feel this even more strongly than we know. If this fits in with a congregation's idea that the minister is, by definition, someone they can call up at any and every moment then the stage is set for this scene to be repeatedly and continuously played out — even if it is obvious to an outside, disinterested party that both demand and effort go way beyond the borders of real need and expectation. Moreover, we may also have grown up with some unrecognized need in ourselves to please people. This can lead to us getting into the position of never being able to say 'No', be angry, or upset anyone. We will be in trouble if we have a congregation which, in turn, demands to be pleased and not disagreed with. The interaction of pressure from without and within us sets up a strain that can become too much.

Any lasting change in these sorts of situations can only be brought about if we can become more aware and understanding of the powerful hidden pressures that may be operating. It then becomes more possible for us to exercise a freer *choice* as to how we respond. That choice *is* a real one. It seems to me quite possible for us to understand more of what goes on in ourselves, the internal drives and pressures that impel us towards certain courses of action such as overwork, and still decide to make that choice just because it fits with what to us is a 'higher' value, that of the gospel to which we are committed. Whether that choice — to overwork — would be made so often with more understanding must remain an open question. But the point I am wanting to emphasize at this moment is that in the area of religion and ministry there is an inherent pressure that is not present for other caring professions, *per se*. It is that of interpreting and internalizing the values of the gospel or other religious tradition, which can at some points seem to fly in the face of both common sense and human well-being.

I do not want to duck this issue for I believe it to be vital in a book whose particular context is not merely the underlying psychology of religion, but rather the *dialogue* between this and the content and values of the religious tradition. In order to begin to illustrate some of this I shall end this chapter with five imaginary case histories of people who, from now on, are going to appear and reappear. These case histories are imaginary, and are not directly based on real individuals. But the situations and experiences they describe are all drawn from real life. They are deliberately taken from different traditions, and from different ministerial situations.

I cannot at this point of first meeting begin to give, or perhaps even claim to know, the complete 'story' of these five imaginary people, just as when we first meet a real person we cannot know everything that 'makes them tick'. As we get to know them better so we can come to understand them more, and this is what I hope will happen with these five people as their stories unfold in the following pages.

John

John is thirty-one and single; he was nicknamed 'The Beanstalk' throughout his schooldays, and looking at his 6ft 3in height and thin, spare frame, we can see why. He tends to go about his parish in his black cassock; it suits his religious persuasion, his pocket and his inner sense that he doesn't want to be bothering with a lot of clothes. But it does accentuate the general witch-on-a-broomstick effect! He was ordained eight years ago, did a long stint as a curate in his first parish, and then moved to take independent charge of this one. But he is not formally and indestructibly 'the vicar', for the 'parson's freehold' was suspended a few years ago in a diocesan reorganization.

An aerial view of his 'patch' would show a multitude of high-rise flats, some open ground which on closer inspection turns out to be partly genuine green park and partly disused land around derelict buildings: warehouses and the like. Dotted around are clusters of smallish Victorian houses, some terraced, some detached; many of these have been attractively done up but contrast sharply with the rather run-down look of the estates. Closer up still it becomes obvious that the population is multi-ethnic, multi-aged and differentially endowed with this world's goods. John knows that there is actually a lot of poverty, overcrowding and homelessness.

The church is neo-Gothic and difficult to heat, with a rose window of some distinction. That rose window keeps John awake at nights! It badly needs restoring for both structural and aesthetic reasons, but how to pay for this? The fifty or so people, including families, who come regularly to Sunday services rattle about in a space designed to hold a large nineteenth-century congregation. It's pretty hard too to develop any lay leadership; the regular congregation prefer to be led rather than goaded into responsibility

Over the years John has wondered increasingly what exactly his job is and how well he can possibly be doing it. Should he become identified with or even take stands for and against the various social and political issues that are always surfacing in this area, or should he 'keep himself (and the Church) to himself'?

The obvious clergy functions of regular services, weddings and funerals take up disproportionately little of his time, yet he senses that his congregation and others expect quite a lot from him; the problem is that it is difficult to see quite what. Furthermore, as a whole they are not always very grateful for what he does do. He is forever hearing variations on the theme of: 'Can't you do something about the cold in the Church? . . . I phoned you yesterday and you weren't in . . . I didn't like last Sunday's form of service when the children made such a noise — can't we go back to three separate services?' This rather carping attitude is not, however, universal. There is a small number of women in the parish who seem to have become attached to him in a way that he cannot really understand and finds difficult. For these people he can do no wrong, but they make inordinate demands on his time and attention — from requests to hear their confessions and repeated invitations to meals that are too big and take too long, to embarrassingly large presents at Christmas and other times.

John is by nature conscientious; he has always worked hard, getting up early and going to bed late. For him it is almost an article of faith that his vicarage should be 'open house'. His day off is theoretically Monday, but theoretically is the word. Last Monday he had a meeting of his (small) PCC, the one before that the Social Services descended on him with a housing problem, and a distressed parishioner has just rung up to ask if she can see him urgently this coming Monday.

To John's horror the job is beginning to feel a burden. In part he would like to be less responsible, take more time off and even dodge parishioners and their demands. But at the same time, and in a strange contradiction, he finds himself redoubling his efforts and scolding himself inwardly when he flags. In addition, he feels less sure of the relevance of his training to the situation in which he finds himself, and this breeds a resentment in him. And, as if this was not enough, the familiar discipline of prayer has become harder: better, he feels, to snatch another hour in bed than to heave himself into church for a blank hour trying to concentrate on God but being plagued by such thoughts as 'What's it all about?; Is it all worth it?; What do I believe anyway?'.

He begins to feel the physical effects of overwork: tension, tiredness and a sense of edgy irritability. After some months of this an old tummy ulcer which first emerged in his pre-finals term at university flares again. He has no option but to consult the doctor, who pronounces that he is suffering from 'stress', dispatches him to the hospital for tests and puts him off sick for a fortnight, though let it be said here that it's quite hard to be off sick when living alone *and* on the job!

If we probe John's background a little more, we learn that he is an only child, born rather late on. His father worked long hours and sometimes shift work in the shipbuilding industry, and was not often around. As a child John sensed that his mother was not very happy. She moved around edgily, rather as he does now, and sometimes he caught her in tears. She fussed over him in a strange sort of way. He was bright, travelled further to school than most of the children in the neighbourhood and had more homework, which he and his mother agonized over — usually to little effect. She never talked after this sort of encounter but just looked at him with sad, worried eyes. The only time she really came into her own was when he was ill — lots of fussing over every little sneeze: You'll get bronchitis or pneumonia; you mustn't go to school today. But at least when he wasn't well he *felt* she cared for him, whilst when he was well and, later, branching out they seemed to live in different worlds with a huge gulf between them. Illness she understood; feelings and ideas she couldn't.

Anne

Anne is small, dark and inclined to be on the plump side. She might be anything from thirty-five to fifty (actually she is forty-four). You might or might not guess that she is a Catholic nun, for she wears nothing to distinguish her as a Religious. In fact, she isn't technically a nun as her order has never been enclosed in solemn vows — she is a Religious Sister, but to most people that is a nicety. Possibly not to Anne herself, for it may affect how she thinks deep inside about her vows.

Anne entered her order straight from her convent school. At the time it seemed natural, even inevitable, for the nuns who taught her always seemed somehow to convey the message that no lesser sacrifice would do. The first years were rather like school with a lot more added on in terms of prayer, discipline and what was called 'mortification'. In fact this meant giving up the things you most liked and even denying that you liked them. She swapped school uniform for a full, traditional habit, very hot in summer but actually rather becoming to her, though that thought would certainly have been sinful. After two years enclosed in an intensive novitiate she was trained for teaching, as indeed were all the sisters, regardless of their aptitude or otherwise. Rumour had it that several sisters had difficulty with their classes but rumour it remained for no one would actually talk about it.

The late 1960s, though, saw a near revolution in convent life. Habits were first shortened and modified, then abandoned. The second Vatican Council had suggested it, and on the grapevine it was said it had come to a head in their own community when one of the sisters had an accident in the car because of not being able to see sideways properly. In a few years all but the very old sisters were in 'ordinary' clothes, except they tended to look a bit dowdy. With ordinary clothes came ordinary houses — goodbye to the endless corridors and dark green paint — and living in small groups of six to ten rather than fifty to sixty. Changes too in work; over time Anne's order gave up their own schools and teacher training colleges and increasingly more sisters, including Anne herself, were employed by local authorities in the State system.

At first Anne, carried along by the reforming spirit of Vatican II, welcomed these changes: 'More sensible, more economic, nearer to the vision of the Foundress, and, above all, more natural and human . . .' New vistas opened up, part of a world she thought she'd given up and forgotten.

But two years ago everything started to go wrong. Anne applied for and got (against some quite stiff competition from lay teachers) a post in a large comprehensive. But this meant larger classes and discipline problems. Many of the children just seem not to want to learn anything. What, too, has her convent background taught her that will help her cope with what she suspects are many children's home situations? Twice in one term girls had to leave because of pregnancy, and only last week an eleven-year-old boy broke down in class because he couldn't bear the violent rows at home and the constant fear of his parents splitting up. How do you cope with a boy in tears, stop some of the others from getting at him *and* teach your class, all at the same time? How, too, do you cope with insolent and obscene language and the threat of violent behaviour. 'In our schools it just wouldn't happen,' comes out from Anne in a mixture of fear and quite 'unreligious' anger, 'or at least not to your face.' Here she discounts the earlier shadowy rumours that sometimes it did.

Judging by the conversation in the large mixed staffroom these sorts of episodes happen quite often. Others on the staff recover by letting off steam: 'Those little . . .s'. In a way Anne would like to feel included — she needs to let off steam too — but is shocked by both language and sentiments; so she remains outside but can't help listening. She has a dialogue only with herself.

Her inner dialogue goes something like this: 'I ought to be coping better, people expect me to . . . I'm too shy to talk here, especially to all those men, *and* I feel like a fish out of water with the *way* they all talk. Anyway I think they think I'm stand-offish and unfriendly because I dont stay on to things or even to talk . . . I can't, I'm a nun and I have to be back in my community.'

In fact Anne never checks out this last point. She *assumes* the other sisters wouldn't like it if she stayed longer at school. But going back home provides little respite for, and the very thought makes her cringe, Sheila will be there, as always. Sheila is another sister belonging to her group of six, younger than Anne by thirteen years, apparently having no trouble in her school. In polite terms they find each other difficult; less politely, they hate each other's guts, if Anne could allow herself to think in those terms. Sheila *can,* apparently — only yesterday she came out with 'you irritate me so much sometimes I could scream'. All Anne can do is withdraw into herself and go silent, even though right inside something else rises up: 'How dare you, can't you realize it's you who are irritating, coming in from school moaning you're tired, expecting to be waited on hand and foot . . . you're just like Maureen was.'

To find out who Maureen is we have to go back a long way. Maureen is Anne's unfavourite younger sister. Anne herself is the eldest of a large family and from aged nine on was often left to look after her younger brothers and sisters. Maureen led her a complete dance — rude, spoilt, said she hated Anne, caused havoc and yet cunningly managed to be out of the way when parental wrath descended. There was more too; as devout Catholics Anne's parents half expected, half wanted a nun or a priest from among their children. Yet that wasn't quite the whole story — in amongst the pride there was also the thought: 'Who will look after the others when you've gone, yet we can't mind really because of your vocation. But just mind you're a good nun for us.' Anne came to feel that she owed it to them as well as to God to be the most perfect Religious she could, and at least, she added to herself, 'I shall be away from Maureen.'

But twenty-five years later she isn't, and indeed there's no chance of getting away from this Maureen (not that Anne herself really sees the connection all that well across the years and different worlds). At least under the old regime the rule of silence and the size of the community would have kept them apart, but not here. Irrational anger and near hate flare, *but* 'put up with it, embrace it and use it as material for intercessory prayer' says the theory of the religious life. Yet still it comes inside: 'I can't stand her any more, I wish she'd fall under the nearest bus . . . God, stop me having such a dreadful thought . . .'

After nearly two years of struggling, both at home and at

school, Anne is nearly on her beam ends. She is tired to the point of having to drag herself around, dreading going to school and dreading coming home again, wishing every night for sleep that doesn't come or, if it does, is just a temporary respite before the dark pit feeling of the next morning. It feels at one and the same time like a great load and a great emptiness. 'This can't be me, it must be the menopause' — yet more darkness, more exhaustion. And, in the middle of the night: 'I can't go on, I'm so bad and awful inside, I must be in the wrong place, yet I can't leave. Can this life or any life be meant to be like this?'

All this goes on locked up inside Anne. Luckily — to her way of seeing things — no one else seems aware of it until one day she has a totally uncharacteristic outburst of anger in her community. It is only after this that her Superior becomes concerned for her and asks, 'Why didn't you say you've been so depressed?'

Peter

From Anne's community we travel apparently several light-years into the heart of Peter and his wife Jane's family life. Here, in a rather-too-small house in the suburb of a northern industrial city there is not even a pretence at peace and quiet. The pair have been bickering for several months and angry eruptions are becoming more frequent.

There is a lot going on for them. Peter is a Free Church minister, and it looks as if he is likely to be moved to yet another congregation in the next year or two. He's heard rumblings that six years is thought to be getting rather a long time . . . Jane went back to nursing recently; she wanted to, and anyway she maintains she had to because of the financial strain of two near-teenage boys. For Peter and the boys this has been a bit of a rude awakening. Mum isn't always around when they want her; the washing up doesn't just go away, and it's no longer any use hoping that unexpected meals or extra clean clothes will always be there on tap. It all needs more planning and pulling together and that's asking a bit much sometimes — especially now.

The move? Almost unbearable to think of right in the middle of the children's education. It will be the third in thirteen years. Another three months or more living in and out of boxes — and the curtains and the furniture almost certainly wouldn't fit somewhere new. 'It wouldn't be so bad if we had at least *somewhere* we could call our own' . . . but the rub is that they haven't, and aren't likely to have for several years, if ever. Even the smallest cottage anywhere is out of bounds financially.

And two weeks ago the unthinkable worst happened. Jonathan, the eldest boy, came home with a policeman — in full view of the neighbours — having been caught with a friend pinching sweets from the shop. Nothing more than a caution happened this time, but the shock and shame were terrible. The minister's son getting into that sort of trouble . . .

Peter, in particular, finds himself regarding his son with almost, if he dare admit it, feelings of disgust and hatred. He has completely forgotten the incident in his own childhood when he was thrashed by his father for telling a lie about something he had done at school, and forgotten also the fierce humiliation he had felt at the time. To make matters worse, Jonathan, instead of being sorry, seems sullen and defiant about it all, muttering things like 'well, if *you* had to have a minister as a father'.

This is the sort of time when parents really need to sit down to relate and talk, but they can't. On a normal day one comes in almost as the other goes out. The only time they are certain to meet is at night in bed, but with all the frayed edges around, their sexual life, like everything else, is suffering.

The bickering came to one of its increasingly frequent heads yesterday when Jane erupted at Peter and threw at him that she was utterly fed up with being married to the church building, congregation and God, and that if Peter didn't make some changes she was really feeling that they couldn't go on together. She added, seemingly rather spitefully, that Peter has been visiting a particular recently-widowed parishioner so often lately that she is beginning to wonder if there is something between them.

This is the strongest outburst so far and it stuns Peter. He feels both the injustice — that it *all* seems to be being made his fault — and also the potential shame of separation or divorce which would make it impossible for him to continue his ministry. The faces of various 'respectable' members of his congregation flash in and out of his mind with despair as he visualizes their reaction to his son being caught by the police *and* his marriage going on the rocks. His fantasies go quite out of hand as he imagines them informing the local press, asking for his immediate removal from his church, and blacking him from all future short lists.

Quite apart from this he loves his wife and values his marriage. In a moment of part awareness, part self-pity and part self-recrimination he upbraids himself: perhaps he did take Jane a bit too much for granted in the early years, thinking she would be glad to share his vocation — after all, hadn't his mother always been delighted at all his enterprises? Then self-justification quickly reasserts itself, for had he not accepted willingly enough the idea of Jane working full-time, even though this meant that he has had to take more share in the running of the home than ideally he has time for, or his own family background would have inclined him to expect. In and amongst his hurt he is deeply angry that she does not seem to appreciate this.

Elizabeth

Elizabeth is twenty-nine, licensed to work in the Anglican church for the last three years and about to be ordained deacon. She lives and works in a large suburban parish. A large chunk of her time is taken up with responsibility for young people; that's tradition; all the women workers before her have done this. But the team ministry has moved on with the times so that they all, including Elizabeth, also have a geographical patch of their own to look after. In this way teaching, preaching and counselling have come her way in abundance.

But the rub is the sacraments. For communion, confession and marriage Elizabeth has to call in one of the men. *She* doesn't like it, '*her*' parishioners don't like it and neither actually do the men. To them it's rather a chore, and they have plenty to do in their own quarter. Funerals are permitted her, and she thinks rather wryly when officiating at them, 'They only trust us with the dead, not the living, and what sort of a slant on ministry is this?'.

Elizabeth, though, is normally philosophical and equable,

on the lines of the prayer about changing what can be changed and having the wisdom to know what can't! She knew when she went into it the position of women's ministry in the Church of England. That's partly why her colleagues like her, and are able to be understanding and even indignant on her behalf; she doesn't spend her time rocking the boat and making a lot of fuss and bother about it. Neither she nor they imagine that there may be a bonfire of disappointment and resentment slowly smouldering away in the depths of her inside self. But of late, even though accepting the latest setbacks in the movement towards the ordination of women, the bonfire has shown signs of life. More of her time and more of her energy now go into meeting and talking with those groups who, sometimes quietly and sometimes very vociferously, feel an urgent pressure to move the process forward.

Last year was fraught: Elizabeth's father died. They'd always been very close and the loss was totally unexpected. Illness, death and funerals always mean a lot of family contact, often between people who don't usually get on or see much of each other. Elizabeth has this sort of relationship with her married brother. Helping her mother sort out her father's things day off after day off was itself bad enough, but to have to do it in the close proximity of brother Andrew was worse. Those irritating and hurtful asides . . . 'About time you got married isn't it, or are you stuck in that church job of yours?', and more of the same.

Right into the middle of this floated a brand new curate, all fresh from theological college and *very* young! Given all that energy obviously he should share in the youth work — at least for a while to get experience. And of course at the end of the year the inevitable happened: his priesting, and by a strange or not so strange coincidence, there came the promotion of the senior team vicar to an incumbency. And out of the blue, in fact during the ordination service itself, frustration and jealousy hit Elizabeth amidships, and these of a strength and quality she would not before have believed possible.

Elizabeth's equable temperament fails. She can't get back her sense of balance and perspective, makes uncharacteristically nasty remarks at staff meetings, and quarrels over the youth work. People in her patch have often said they wished she could celebrate at the main service. Normally this makes her feel good and valued inside; now the fact that she can't just fuels the fire of her fury.

Where do you go at these sorts of moments when you feel that if you don't get it out somehow you'll burst? Elizabeth tries her boss — the team Rector — to no avail. He can't get the message at all; just looks at her, first confusedly and then in a businesslike way saying, in effect: 'This is unlike you to let this sort of thing get to you. Surely you know what a good job you're doing. I shouldn't worry, it'll be water under the bridge soon . . .'

Things have now got to the stage where Elizabeth has only to look at her younger colleague and she starts mentally making wax images and sticking not pins but large poisonous nails into him. Maybe she's going to have to get out . . . but to where? Hospital chaplaincy? University chaplaincy? They can only be temporary. Another parish? But the same thing will happen again.

A day or two later, Elizabeth tells herself with ever-increasing intensity: 'This really can't go on. Calm down or get out.' Then, 'Pray about it, get forgiveness, perhaps you even need exorcism from the evil state you've got into; go and work abroad, leave the ministry, leave the Church, leave God before He really leaves you'. . . in Elizabeth's inner thoughts a cycle of increasingly wild and improbable fantasies sets up. Yet still there is the deeper down fear: 'What if these feelings never go away, and I'm left without a job, home or anything?'

By an enormous act of will Elizabeth reasserts her usual calm and rationality, and suppresses a nasty feeling each time it rears its head. Prayer seems to work and almost miraculously, it seems, the feelings fade away — until one Friday evening in the crowded supermarket. Out of the blue — at least to her mind — she begins to feel panicky, hot, faint and sick. She thinks for one awful moment that she isn't really there at all or is going mad. By hanging on to the nearest shelf for ten minutes and trying to act normally the panic gradually abates. But the memory remains and the fear that it will happen again, without, as she sees it, any warning.

All the old feelings are coming back as well, and she wonders desperately what she can do or whom she can turn to to help her make sense of it all and stop her feeling that she is going to bits.

Robert

Robert, when we meet him, is walking home to his vicarage having been out and about in his parish. He'd like to have stayed out longer — the weather is nice and he's already bumped into several people he needed to see — but a 'higher' duty calls in the shape of a pre-arranged visit from the archdeacon. When he rang to make the appointment the archdeacon said that the bishop thinks that he, Robert, might like to go on an in-service training course for mature men seeking to reflect on the development of their ministry. The meeting is to talk about this and, if appropriate, make some practical arrangements for the charge of his parish whilst he's away.

Robert is actually fifty-seven, so he supposes wryly that this may make him mature! As he approaches his vicarage he takes stock briefly of himself and his situation. Three children; one married, the other two at university and going through the throes of the job market but with good prospects. A wife; happy in the parish, busier possibly even than he. This reminds him that he has to pick her up from her meeting with the fund-raising group in a couple of hours' time. It behoves him to get rid of the Archdeacon in good time so that he's not late, otherwise he'll hear about it for some time! Happily married for twenty-five plus years . . . An Anglican parish in rural England, no curates, thank goodness. At fifty-seven there will be no need for him to move again; he can stay here for the rest of his active ministry. All quite satisfactory, he thinks as he looks out beyond the last houses of the village to the countryside. All satisfactory, all quite peaceful, except for the infernal noise of that wretched tractor a couple of fields away.

Or at least it would all be satisfactory if *they,* namely the bishop and the archdeacon, would just let him be and stop suggesting things like in-service courses and hinting at new initiatives and responsibilities. He gathers that they really

want him for rural dean. Why he cannot think, as he himself
is quite resigned to not getting any further up the Church's
ladder. In fact he does not even see it as a ladder; he has no
ambition; his vocation is quite enough for him, as it should be
for everyone else. Yvonne, his wife, agrees with him, and
indeed he senses that she would get impatient if he showed
any signs of restlessness.

His attention wanders from his surroundings as suddenly
he finds himself contemplating the mental picture of his
brother, who is a very successful stockbroker in the City. In
an off-key moment he might have described him as 'the rat
race personified'. His thoughts pass on, out of his control, to
his memory of a recent, rather strange conversation, when his
brother had mused aloud: 'It's funny, our lives have gone so
differently. I always thought you'd be in quite a different job
and position. I never really saw you as a vicar and certainly
not settling for a parish like this, especially after all the
interesting work you were doing in your last job in the middle
of Birmingham. I know that didn't quite work out in the end,
that it folded when the congregation complained at the
experiment of trying to share the church building with the
Islamic community . . . but . . .'

Robert remembers laughing this off with words to the
effect that he's forsaken the desire to get on in the world, and
really he is very content and happy where he is. He'd be
happy to cut off his reflections here — again it's all quite
satisfactory, — but unaccountably they go on a bit. He *has*
had, it's true, vague twinges of hurt about the Birmingham
affair, but these do not last. He also occasionally has the
sense that it's difficult to go on being creative in sermons, and
there's a certain sameness and dullness about the liturgy that
used not to be there. He doesn't always feel very energetic
and some of the hobbies he used to enjoy such as walking
and painting don't seem to attract him so much now, but
there's nothing really wrong. Except that the wretched bishop
and the archdeacon seem to fuss about how he is and what
he's doing. If only they would leave him alone . . .

He supposes that their concern is all part of the new drive
towards 'support'. It's even been suggested that he might like
to join a diocesan group of clergy who meet to share their
difficulties together. Why? He doesn't actually have any and

his theological training led him to understand that ministry would sometimes be dull and even tiring and that this is to be expected. The thing to do with difficulties, he sermonizes to himself, is to pray about them and ask for strength; but anyway he *really* does not have any. He remembers from childhood that you don't make a fuss or bother about any little trifle that doesn't go quite right; mother was always too busy and rather impatient, and father would have laughed at his getting upset. In fact the Bishop's attitude is confusing and irritating, and he doesn't quite know how to take it. Is there something behind it which he hasn't picked up? Is he somehow being got at?

On that not very auspicious note Robert comes to himself, looks at his watch, starts at the time and reluctantly heads for the garden gate and the house. He needs to make sure there is tea or coffee for the Archdeacon, who is now due to arrive in less than ten minutes' time!

These five people are all suffering strain and have got to the stage — even Robert, though he does not know it — where they need some support and help. Otherwise, John may remain physically ill and require ever-increasing medical investigation and treatment; Anne could go deeper into depression and even suicide; Peter and Jane's marriage could break up or their son become more antisocial or delinquent; Elizabeth could find it increasingly difficult to function in her role if she continues to have panic attacks; and Robert may well become more and more withdrawn and never realize any more of his potential.

Many manifestations of strain and stress may not be as obvious as these. In some ways it may be good for John, Anne, Peter and Elizabeth that they are experiencing them in their more acute forms as they may feel pressed to do something about it. Others, like Robert, may go on for months or years not really knowing that something is wrong, though they get some sense of it from time to time. But even then they cannot put a name to it, let alone ask for help.

In these people we see, as it were, the tip of an iceberg. They are in bad trouble and the trouble is showing. We are unlikely to be able to identify entirely with their stories, but in probability a part of them is a part of all of us in similar positions. We all need self-awareness and support both to avoid comparable disaster and to realize our creative potential.

The question that then arises is, 'Where can support be found?' For these people at this point it may well have to be found professionally, but in the long term we have to ask questions about the supportiveness or otherwise of the system and situation of which they are all a part. It is, therefore, an appraisal of this aspect of ministry to which we turn in the next chapter.

Notes

1. 2 Corinthians 11.28.
2. John 14.1.
3. Luke 12.25–6, 32.
4. See, for example, articles and letters in the *Church Times:* deserted clergy wives, 16 August 1985; low income, 21 August 1987; job-finding, 3, 28 October 1986.
5. Diocese of Bath and Wells, Ministry Commission, July 1983.
6. Report from House of Bishops to the General Synod of the Church of England, August 1985.
7. George Reindorp *No Common Task,* Hodder and Stoughton 1957.
8. R. J. Bocock 'The Role of the Anglican Clergyman', *Social Compass,* 17(4) 1970, pp. 533–44.
9. More recently there has been renewed work on identifying skills essential and specific to pastoral care. See L. Virgo, ed. *First Aid in Pastoral Care,* T & T Clark 1987. Training courses in pastoral care have been set up, and the Association for Pastoral Care and Counselling is addressing this issue directly (in a Consultation, January 1988 — see *APCC Journal,* Summer 1988).
10. For fuller treatment of this issue see Chapter 10 on sources of support and ways of providing it.
11. In, for example, courses for senior Church leaders held at St George's House, Windsor Castle.
12. Romans 7.19.

TWO

Setting the Scene

We ended the last chapter with five people in distress, and we learned quite a lot about their personal circumstances, past and present. But in concentrating on beginning to get to know them as individual people we could not pay proper attention to another dimension; they *are* unique individuals, but they do not live in a vacuum. Other people, such as Anne's Superior and fellow sisters, Peter's son, Elizabeth's colleagues and Robert's brother and Bishop come in and out of their stories and make a significant contribution. Furthermore, they all come to us out of 'something' and 'somewhere'.

It is this 'something' and 'somewhere' that I want to examine in this chapter. It is a mammoth task, rather like trying to take a photograph or film of a very rich and varied subject. To focus on one part that seems very important and to bring it into sharp relief inevitably means that, even with the most sophisticated camera, something else will go out of perspective. And my 'camera', that is, my selective and reflective capacity, is not nearly as foolproof as the technological equivalent. Nevertheless, unless we at least attempt to take the photo, *nothing* can be captured.

So, how do we start? One way to get into the scene is to take a short film of what these people are actually up to in their ministry and use this as a starting point. It would take too long to film them all so I am going to select one only, knowing that patterns of ministry vary, but hoping that there is enough common ground for issues that emerge from one study to enable a more general reflection.

I would like to portray John's way of life through thirty-six hours from a Friday afternoon to Saturday night/Sunday morning. I am going to work through his diary, inevitably

32

from 'outside' but at times letting some of his own thoughts come through.

John isn't looking forward to this particular Friday afternoon. He has a funeral and then a school governors' meeting, and both occasions promise to be fraught. If he'd had a choice he'd never have put them on the same day, but then people don't choose when to die!

Feelings in the neighbourhood are running high about this funeral, mostly against the local services and the Government. The deceased, an elderly man of seventy-nine, fell in his flat, broke a hip, wasn't found for two days and subsequently died in hospital from pneumonia. He'd been sent home from the same hospital only four months ago pending the finding of sheltered accommmodation. Everybody 'knew' he should never have been sent home and everybody is furious and prepared, for once, to be at the funeral to make the point. They temporarily 'forget' that they had all stopped visiting, even John himself when he comes to think about it, because the man was so unwelcoming. If he himself is anything to go by, everybody is also feeling rather guilty and not prepared to admit this — better to blame the social services who admittedly do seem to have taken their time.

Everybody expects something from John in his address, yet it's a minefield. If he says too much, he'll lose his working relationship with the local services; if he says too little, he'll have the neighbourhood banging on his door shouting that they thought Christianity was about caring for the poor. All this quite apart from the fact that a funeral service is meant to commend somebody to God, not be a political forum . . . particularly as the old man's daughter was very upset when John saw her this morning; she knows she hasn't been near him and now feels awful about this.

Then the governors' meeting. John curses the custom that makes the vicar ex-officio chairman of the governing body of a Church school in that strange system whereby the Established Church cohabits with the State, sometimes rather uneasily. Chairmanship skills were not part of his theological college syllabus. On today's agenda the two main items are the state of the boiler and the complaint of a parent against a teacher for alleged racist remarks. The first he could do without for he has enough trouble with the church boiler; the second is a very hot potato, particularly in this neighbourhood . . .

5.30 p.m. Back home, thank goodness; feeling really drained . . . still he survived.

6.00 p.m. Evensong in church with two of the faithful. ('Can I go out the vestry door afterwards to dodge them?' Better not, so caught in conversation for twenty minutes.)

6.45 p.m. Home and the phone rings. Another parishioner . . . can she talk to him urgently about what's going on with her family? Could it be this evening because of everyone being at home over the weekend? ('I can't stand it, perhaps Monday — I know it's my day off, but I really should have said "Yes" for this evening'.)

7.00 p.m. Supper. ('Stomach churning a bit so be careful about what to eat.')

It's the sort of evening when John would really like not to be alone; the afternoon is still 'inside' him a bit, but there it is, he has to be. ('Start on Sunday's sermon perhaps . . . Oh, no, I'd forgotten that Trinity Sunday has such impossible readings . . . the choice of the vision of the Lord high and lifted up, or lofty parts of St Paul and St John . . . to make something of these for adults *and* children? . . . No, not tonight.')

Desultory reading, a couple of whiskies — one more than he really meant to have — and bed.

9.00 a.m. Saturday. Matins — later than usual, thank goodness, because it's Saturday — no congregation. The all too familiar routine has little meaning for John this morning, but at least he's fulfilled his obligation.

10.30 a.m. Confirmation class at the vicarage which he enjoys; this is what he was ordained for, and he has the biggest group of children he's ever had. They seem to enjoy it too . . .

11.30 a.m. Shopping: crowded as always on a Saturday but must have food for next week. Delay at supermarket checkout means no real time for a snack before . . .

1.00 p.m. and 2.30 p.m. Two weddings. Not people he knows personally except for one preparation interview. The same set of hymns twice over . . . ('Important to try to make this a meaningful occasion for bride and groom and guests . . . not easy, though.')

4.00 p.m. Back home and some time off except for that wretched sermon. Sit at the Amstrad for inspiration . . . Tramp at the door, providing an excuse to knock off . . . ('No point in trying to get back to it now; how can anyone preach about the Trinity? I can't really think about it myself . . . at least I'm out this evening, so there's no need to think about food.')

5.30 p.m. Phone call from the Area Dean. Can he take some services over the next month in the next-door parish. Vicar ill and non-stipendiary minister can't cover everything. ('*That* vicar ill and strained . . . what does he think I am?') says John resentfully after putting the phone down and looking at his now over full diary.

Evening out with friends — good chance to relax, but can't stay too late because of the sermon.

12.30 a.m. Sermon will have to do . . . Sunday ahead. ('8.30 a.m. *and* 10.30 a.m. Holy Communion services . . . still haven't persuaded the 8 o'clock remnant to cope with the Parish Communion . . . Bother, the cat's at the back door; what with the sermon must have forgotten to let it in . . . just hope that meal doesn't stop me sleeping or play havoc with my stomach . . .')

What can we learn from this short sequence of John's life about the 'soil' in which he and other ministers are embedded?

John functions as the representative leader of the Church, the religious community. That much is easy to see from the catalogue of preaching, teaching, responding to pastoral calls and officiating at services and sacraments. In these it is not just the present day that counts; he, and the Church, exist within a historical heritage, of which his struggle to translate the biblical readings for Trinity Sunday into something meaningful to his congregation is an obvious example.

Yet we see also how the Church cannot live for itself alone. A funeral and a school governors' meeting bring John and the Church into relationship, dialogue and possibly conflict with the total community; he cannot escape from the issue of the quality of care in the community nor that of racial equality. Furthermore, as I, and perhaps he, reflect on his two weddings, the question pops up 'why did *they* want to be married in church?'; what does the Church stand for to those who live on its boundary — mostly outside, sometimes just inside?

And every so often we see glimpses of John not as *the minister* but as an ordinary human being who has to eat, shop, let the cat in and who is subject to moments of loneliness, irritation and the rest.

The 'something' and 'somewhere' out of which ministers come is beginning to acquire some shape. We can, I think, see ourselves as living at the intersection of our present situation — that is as representatives of the religious institutions which themselves have to relate to the wider community — with the religious tradition. Moreover, we live at that intersection point with all the resources, weaknesses and complexities which characterize us as human beings.

Two things immediately strike me. First, the order I found myself choosing in the last paragraph is itself interesting, and has important implications for much of what follows. The question that emerges is simple: is a minister or Religious — either to himself or herself or to others — first or last a human being? I well remember, during my early years as a Religious, being on holiday in my home village dressed in the traditional habit. Whilst walking down the road towards a group of children playing together I was aghast to find that they scattered hastily at my approach. Worse, I saw one of them rush into his house in some distress, and heard him call out to his mother, 'Mummy, there's something dreadful in the road, and I don't know what it is!' This is a somewhat extreme example of a dehumanizing process that often seems to attend ministers and pastors; many others could relate similar experiences. The stories are usually told for entertainment and seen as basically very funny, but they mask a disturbing thought: Is there something we do to ourselves, as ministers, or allow others to do to us which somehow clothes us in the symbolic equivalent of a novice's habit and cuts us off from the human race? If this is so, why does it happen; what sort of unacknowledged hopes, fears and fantasies go into the process? These are questions that we are not yet ready to assess, but I hope we may be able to do so as this book proceeds.

Our humanness is universal; our religious context, past and present, is particular, relating to *a* dimension of our being. Yet in this statement is 'begged' one of the greatest questions. *Can* we separate the religious dimension from our humanness in this way? Should we try to discover how human beings tick from *within* the overarching belief — which has to be of faith not knowledge — that to be human is to be related to God, or do we leave that as an open question as we observe and explore our human development?

In keeping faith with the Preface I shall leave that question unanswered, and try, rather, to go freely into both dimensions, knowing and accepting that they cannot be independent, yet trying not to look at each only from the vantage (i.e. *ad*vantage) point of a foothold within the other. To an extent this must fail for I come to this reflection, as does the reader, from a particular, if ever-changing, point of involvement with the question, but I do not think that this invalidates the attempt.

The minister as the representative of a religious institution

My richest source of material for this part of my reflection is the Christian Church, though I have the Jewish community also in mind. The two institutions obviously have similarities that may be greater than those between either of them and any non-religious institution, but they also have differences which need to be borne in mind.

There are two factors inherent in the nature of the Church which seem to be particularly relevant to the whole question of stress in ministry.

(1) *The Church or religious body as care-giver*

To a greater or lesser extent the religious body is seen as offering unlimited care; indeed we use the metaphor and symbol of Mother Church with all its overtones of maternal care and nurture. In concrete terms, this offer is greatest in the established Church of England which has, at least in theory, a wider role than any other religious body in Britain, with anyone being able to call upon its services, and least in the Jewish community, which traditionally is more confined to caring for its own people, though Jewish philanthropy, as distinct from pastoral care, has embraced broader aims.

If we now loose the symbol of the maternal care of the religious bodies from its base in geographical Britain and let it 'float free', as it were, we can reflect more easily upon the nature of the associations and expectations it arouses. On some, probably not wholly articulated, level people do seem to associate the Church and indeed any religious community with a duty and capacity for unlimited and unconditional care and altruism. Quite where this idea comes from is not easy, exactly, to establish. Does it come from the use of the symbol 'mother' or has that word merely given a name to what was already there? There is certainly historical precedent in the social and other good works pioneered by religious communities through the ages. Does it stem from the teaching of Jesus,[1] or should it be traced to the sense that care is unlimited and freely given which comes from our apprehension of an omnipotent and unlimited God who has no boundaries of time, space or availability?

Yet *human* space, time and love *are* limited; the incarnation of the care of God in human beings and human institutions, inevitably, cannot reflect the fullness of the bounty of the source. This is obvious on an intellectual level, but on more emotional levels there may arise sharp conflict, disappointment and disillusion bordering on contempt and disgust when religious bodies fail to meet this expectation for unlimited care and altruism. In this context it may be useful to reflect on the way in which Israel continues to be vilified in the international community and the world's press, often portrayed as 'cruel', 'terrorist' or the like. This is not to condone cruelty or terrorism in any form or by any country, but just to ask the question whether there is something in the expectations — invested in Israel as the inheritor of the symbol of the chosen people of God that gives rise to such strong expressions of condemnation when she 'fails'?

Furthermore, past history will not substantiate the fantasy that the religious bodies have been, *in fact,* all-caring. For there have been instances, such as in the time of the Inquisition, when the Christian Church has been anything but caring, when it has been neglectful and persecuting. It seems as if the care of 'Mother' Church can be experienced as absent, conditional, smothering or cruel, as can our experience of human motherhood. This tends to get forgotten.

Care certainly is *a* feature of both Christianity and Judaism, but it is not unmixed with un-caring. To isolate unlimited care and proclaim it as *the* characteristic of a religious outlook on life is to idealize that life. This then becomes absolute in a way that allows no space for the essentially mixed nature of human beings and human institutions, or for exploration of the more difficult question of the nature and quality of the care of God.

(2) *The religious community as the Ark*

There is another way in which we can conceive of the Church, and that is as the Ark of God. To an extent this is paralleled by some of the imagery of Israel in the Old Testament as 'the righteous remnant'.[2] In both cases the underlying motif is the same. The religious community is seen as the depository and guardian of truth, purity and righteousness, as the original Noah stood for the one righteous man in the human race, and more indirectly as representative of the righteousness and holiness of God.[3] Many a controversy in Israel's and Church history has centered on the dilemma posed by apparent untruth — in Christianity normally called heresy — or by obvious sin and impurity existing within the holy and truth-filled body.

In some cases, of which the outlawing of the fourth-century Donatist schism[4] and the Jansenist heresy[5] are two examples, the religious bodies themselves have realized the dangers of identifying themselves with extremes of perfect holiness and truth, though sects and movements on the fringes of the main bodies have not. In fact such extremes lead easily to loss of compassion and love and to an obsession with 'who's in and who's out'. On the whole these extremes have been recognized for what they are — as tending to fanaticism, cruel exclusivism, and to a human disorder in which feelings and thoughts cannot be integrated into a balanced whole.

At less than the extreme pole, however, there is still, *within* both Christianity and Judaism, a strong need to keep the Ark safe, a great hope for security of belief and faith. Much anxiety and hostility is generated when this hope seems to be threatened as can be seen, for example, in the controversies which surrounded the publication of Bishop John Robinson's *Honest to God,*[6] and, more recently, the pronouncements of the Bishop of Durham, David Jenkins.[7]

Into this inheritance ministers must enter, and will be required to personify the faithful Noah. Inevitably they will occupy the front line and will have a symbolic role that goes beyond and is greater than their own individual contribution.

These issues — of care and guardianship — will be taken up in greater detail in Chapters 5, 6 and 7. But they are both inherently part of the context of ministry which particular ministers, with their own special history and circumstances, will enter as they take up their position in the religious community to which they are attached.

The minister in relation to the wider community

The religious bodies, like individuals, do not themselves exist in a vacuum; they are part of the total neighbourhood and nation.

On one level we might think that we are able to abstract them from this total context, at least in connection with the affairs of religion itself. If they *decide* to take a prominent part in the life of the nation this initiative will then appropriately be subject to evaluation, praise and criticism as has indeed been the case over Church pronouncements on such issues as the Bomb or the miners' strike.[8]

We might be forgiven, though, for expecting that, as less than 10 per cent of the population attend church or synagogue regularly, the religious bodies will be left in peace when they are operating within 'their own' sphere and will make little impact on the nation and wider community when operating outside it. For the *overt* attitude among the population is that religion and communities of faith are irrelevant to 'real' life. But this is a very incomplete picture. We have to note occasions such as the defeat of the Sunday Trading Bill[9] when Church bodies have had an effect. We need, too, to acknowledge the continued phenomenon of 'folk' religion. Among the manifestations of this are the greatly increased congregations on Christmas Eve, the great occasions of State such as Remembrance Sunday, and even royal weddings, when the established Church is still seen as 'married' to the State in an apparently quite indissoluble way, and the continuing evidence that the most unlikely people still want to be baptized, married in church and buried according to the rites of religion. There is divided reaction among more committed Church members on this, ranging from all-inclusive acceptance to near all-exclusive rejection. I do not want to go into the pros and cons of this now, but ask rather that we should note what is, on the surface, a rather surprising state of affairs, and begin to explore what may underlie it.

On some level the existence of religion continues to be important to the wider community. Sometimes this level is barely recognized, more often it cannot be articulated, but it is as if the wider community requires the Church and Synagogue — or even Mosque — to be 'there' for it, to serve it, and even in some sense to be 'good' for it, thus possibly allowing society itself to be 'bad'. In this way the religious dimension of life, and its incarnation in actual religious bodies, comes to function as a sort of conscience to the rest of society. It is asked to be a container of other peoples' ideals. These ideals are, so to speak, being 'held' by religion so that they cannot disappear in the inevitable human failure to realize them.

This concept may go some way towards explaining the proprietary attitude sometimes taken by the State, as in the defeat by Parliament of the 1928 revision of the Prayer Book, towards the Church's own reform of its own life. It would also make some sense of the punitive fury that is aroused when a religious body, or a member of it, falls short of the ideal and commits, in particular, a moral offence. Part of this fury may stem from the fear that the container is going to be unequal to its task: perhaps no one will be able to hold goodness and keep it alive for us? Then we should be left at the mercy of badness. In part also the fury could stem from a deep jealousy of the security of faith and existence that the religious bodies purport to offer and their members seem to enjoy, and to which those outside feel they cannot commit themselves. On the surface this is hard to believe, for many people could not easily admit to feeling jealous of those with religious faith; in many ways ridicule is more the order of the day. But opinion polls on the subject of religion have tended to reveal a deep, though rather amorphous, yearning for something of this dimension of meaning.

If indeed this is the case, strange and unpleasant things can follow. People 'outside' feel rage, though they may not realize they feel it, against that exclusive club of those for whom religious faith is meaningful and from which they are excluded — even if in fact they have excluded themselves. This rage gets fuelled if the 'insiders' somehow exude a sense of superiority. Their message can be mixed, even tantalizing: 'You can come in, you can share what we've got, *but only* if you meet our conditions, get baptized, come to church, believe certain things, act in certain ways . . .' In the face of this situation even stranger things happen. The outsiders sometimes idealize the insiders, looking wistfully at these marvellous people who reach a standard they can never reach, or they do an about-turn and denigrate those with faith as 'colourless people, prudes, inadequate, only half-alive'.

It goes, I think, even deeper than this, from jealousy to envy. Jealousy is directed towards people who have what we want and are keeping us out. Envy arises from our relationship with a person or a thing: we want something the other has or is, and when we cannot get it we hate it and want to destroy it. In this context the 'person-thing' is religious faith itself, the security of Mother Church, or God. So the deep, destructive feelings go beyond the people that make up the religious bodies to a hatred of religion itself and of God: 'Religion is punitive and moralistic', 'Christianity is hypocritical', 'the Jewish God is outdated and cruel . . .'

Complications then arise, for we have suggested that on another level these same 'haters' need religion to exist to keep goodness alive for them. So they are in a bind; they suspect they might need something, they don't have it and so in their hate and envy they want to destroy it, but this threatens them in their need for it. So it is better to pull back from destruction of the ultimate ideal and to return to blaming and attacking its various incarnations: 'Religious people don't present religion well enough', 'the Church makes immoral money out of investment and property', 'the Jews are separatist and stand-offish'.

The problem is that there is so often a mixture of distortion *and* a grain of truth in the attacks, and these get very entangled. For the 'attacked' the question has therefore to be, 'Is there any truth here, and if so what can we do about it?'. For the 'attacker' it is, 'What is impelling us to make this sort of attack, and why do we need to?'. Unfortunately, very often neither set of questions gets asked and the tangled knot remains.

Moreover, the attack does not come from one side. The 'attacked' can become the 'attacker'. Let me attempt to illustrate what I mean by an example: in a riot, some people stay apparently unroused on the sidelines, often condemning the violence, whilst in others the violence is increased, almost, it seems, without their conscious consent. It is as if one group disown their violence and, in a strange way, 'put it into'[10] the others. The 'transaction' constitutes a sinister form of attack; the intention was to contain, but the result is inflammation.

This mysterious process can happen in any context, but the religious dimension is vulnerable to becoming an active agent of it to the extent that the vocabulary of religion, and so perhaps its essence, encourages sharp polarisations such as good/bad, violence/peace, light/darkness, holiness/sin. Good people must have only good things inside them, but what then happens to *bad* things?

The whole mechanism may seem quite incredible and is very obscure; we shall explore it anew in the next chapter. Suffice it to say here that we can have evidence, if we look for it, that such 'transfer' processes do happen,[11] and are particularly powerful and primitive when they happen on the large scale, that is within and between large groups and institutions. Then they operate well beyond the apparent capacity of the individual people who constitute such groupings. The emotions generated — which can be positive

or negative — resonate to and are amplified by the situation
in which they emerge.

The existence of these sorts of feelings and forces certainly
complicates the relationship between the religious bodies and
the secular world. As ministers, we stand exposed to this
dimension because of our representative role. So we can get
caught up in the processes, whether they are operating for
good or ill, and it is often very hard to recognize and clarify
what is happening to us. To the extent that we are confused
and disturbed we shall *feel* strained, and there may, indeed,
be much more pressure around than we *can* feel. As anyone
who has ever got a splinter into themselves and not realized it
for a time knows, not all painful and poisoning instrusions
are immediately sensed or easily detectable. This does not
mean, however, that they have not happened.

The minister as inheritor of the biblical tradition

We now turn from the dimension of our present context to
that of our relationship to the religious tradition. I shall here
explore, primarily, the biblical tradition, for I believe this to
be fundamental and to underlie the later developments in
theology.

The biblical images of ministry are several, and not confined
to that of 'priest'. To this we may add 'apostle', 'prophet',
'servant', 'king', and, for those within the Christian tradition,
the image of Christ himself. These images will be there and
stand as part of our inheritance quite independently of the
actual functional state of ministry and the nature and status
of ministerial orders. The images will stand just because they
evoke powerful feelings — some more so than others — and
because they are part of the living Word which in the liturgy,
especially, is re-enacted so as to become part of the
community's internal experience. Ministers will find it hard
to escape from the effects of this inheritance even though
elements of it may well be foreign to their own overt
theological positions. Thus, for example, whether or not a
minister is comfortable with the word or idea of 'priest', with
all its implications in the Old Testament of offering sacrifice,
or acting as the mediator between God and man,[12] the
pressure will be there to represent God to his people and

them to him. The word 'apostle' surely implies something of selectness — being the chosen companion of Christ — sent out and entrusted with the responsibility and leadership of a tremendous mission.[13] 'Prophet' carries the sense of obedience to the word of God, and the requirement to proclaim holiness however unpalatable and unpopular this may be, and whatever the consequences.[14] 'King' at first sight fits less easily with the idea of ministry until we remember the nature of Davidic kingship; here we have the king as the anointed guardian and ruler of the people, the chief agent in the liturgy and the focus of the covenant between God and his people.[15]

These reflections are not in any way esoteric; they derive from a reading of the biblical text with 'ordinary' openness. It does not seem to me difficult to accept that to enter into this kind of inheritance cannot but impose considerable expectation, demand and strain upon the minister. The later doctrine which separated out the efficacy of the work of priesthood from the worthiness or otherwise of the minister[16] can on one level reassure us and take away some of the pressure. But because this reassurance is based on *rational understanding* it will not necessarily remove the pressure from a deeper level of our being.

The images continue to exercise an inordinate pressure on those human beings who fill the actual roles. For Christians they have been further reinforced by the figure of Christ himself.

The person and power of Christ is, to ministers and lay-people alike, at once most reassuring and most threatening. The reassuring side is not too hard to understand; we usually draw on it when we need Christ as 'saviour' standing for and representing God in a way that mediates power and love to us. Threatening is a word not so often used and is one which some may resist and resent. Yet for many of us the imitation of Christ *can* be a threatening challenge — to try to do the impossible, to 'love one another as I have loved you'.[17]

Then we are also inheritors of the biblical tradition on the nature of God the Father. Religious faith proclaims that man is not downed by the majesty and holiness of God but brought to fulfilment and a holiness in himself. But does there not remain a sneaking doubt as to how God, in the Bible, views sin and evil? Can he contain them, as Psalm 139 seems to suggest,[18] or are they necessarily outside his embrace? Either reading brings pressure to ministers; in the first case we are going to be asked to model *his* forgiveness and containment to a degree that will be beyond our human capacity. In the latter we are likely to be expected to reflect an *unalloyed* goodness that again will be impossible for us.

All this constitutes one strand in the biblical tradition, that which emphasizes the *burden* it places on us. But it would be incorrect and unfair to imply by this that the Bible does not recognize nor pay attention to essential humanity and human weakness. We can find many examples in the tradition of human frailty in otherwise great people. In King David's life we have to look no further than his appalling conduct in respect of Uriah the Hittite,[19] whilst Elijah cut a sorry figure of self-pity in the wilderness.[20] Of the shortcomings of the apostles there is no lack of evidence, from Peter's denial to St Paul's very human but hardly edifying outbursts in his letters to the Corinthians.[21]

Here it is important to include another chosen disciple whom many might wish to exclude, although he was one of the Twelve. I am referring, of course, to Judas Iscariot, the betrayer. Yet let it not be forgotten that in the final confrontation in the garden of Gethsemane Jesus still addresses him as 'friend': 'Friend, do you betray the Son of man with a kiss?'[22] Nowhere have some of the implications of this scene been brought out more strongly than in Tim Rice and Andrew Lloyd Webber's musical *Jesus Christ, Superstar* in which the lives of Jesus and Judas are portrayed as being inextricably interwoven, with Judas's growing disillusionment and despair turning to hatred of his one-time hero. In Judas we see the ultimate in human anger and despair, the act of suicide following upon murder, in itself not an uncommon occurrence in today's world. Yet the kiss remains; we cannot cut out Judas any more than we can deny the darker side of human nature. He shows us what humanity includes if we are to take it seriously, and we cannot comfortingly dismiss him from our awareness.

Finally, there is the humanity of Christ. We have seen already how his 'perfectness' can trouble those seeking to imitate him, but we also need to recognize the points at which frailty, weakness and anger come through. He gets tired and a bit impatient, as in the story of the woman at the well in Samaria.[23] He is certainly angry during the cleansing of the Temple,[24] and according to Mark he could have died in despair, for we have no real reason to assume that the quotation of Psalm 22 given in this account — 'My God, my God, why hast thou forsaken me?'[25] — would necessarily have been followed in his mind at the time by the triumphant verses with which the psalm ends.

So the biblical tradition shows us, if we want to see it, the less acceptable face of humanity and of ministry. We can amplify this from later history; even though the biographers of saints display a tendency to portray their subjects through rose-tinted spectacles, in autobiographical writings the not-so-respectable human bits seep through. St Teresa of Avila, in her life and letters, talks of herself as 'half-crazy',[26] and also tells of occasions when her ecstasies had much more of frenzy than of healthy emotional experience about them.[27]

Seventeenth-century Teresa and twentieth-century Thomas Merton,[28] to name but two prominent examples, give much evidence of being under considerable emotional stress. They do not weather it too well either. The question is, How are we to think of their weaknesses, those of the biblical figures and our own humanity?

We can attribute all that 'falls short' of perfection and 'the glory of God'[29] to human sin, and consider all that unpleasantly overtakes us either externally or internally as in some way alien to *true* humanness and to be filtered out of us through the dark night of senses or spirit. On this reading, when faced with the human dilemma articulated by St Paul in his letter to the Romans ('I do not do the good I want, but the evil I do not want is what I do'[30]), we will put our cracks and blemishes down to imperfections in our conversion and sanctification process; somehow the Spirit of God has not been able to have his way with us and we are not converted or religious enough!

Or will we look at an alternative scenario such as is suggested by John Taylor in *The Go-Between God* when he says:

The Spirit is not averse to the elemental world of our dreams, the raw emotion of our fears and angers, the

illogical certainties of our intuitions, the uncharted gropings
of our agnosticism, the compulsive tides of our history.
These are his milieu. [my italics] [31]

The biblical and other tradition is ambivalent here; human
emotions and human not-so-good bits are at least recognized,
not denied, but we cannot gainsay the strong pressure to
transcend rather than to explore them.

The overwhelming sense of this chapter is that the
pressures on ministers from their 'surroundings' are
considerable. Somehow we have to come to terms with
pressures lest they threaten to engulf us.

This is difficult for two reasons. First, we are too much a
part of them to be able to think clearly about them from day
to day. Second, I believe that the main reason why these
pressures are as they are is because *people,* who constitute
the religious bodies and who were responsible for the making
and handing down of the biblical tradition, are as they are. So
it has now become urgent that we take full cognizance of and
try to understand the minister as a human being.

The minister as a human being

We return, belatedly, to the reality of the *person* of the
minister, a human being who is a member of various groups
and who shares in a particular historical and spiritual
inheritance.

We need an understanding of how human beings tick
which I do not think the theological dimension can, of itself,
give us. We are therefore going to have to draw on another
discipline, that of psychology, in order to begin to understand
how we come to be as we are. It is this to which we shall turn
in the next chapter.

Notes

1. For example, the Parable of the Good Samaritan, Luke 10.29ff.
2. e.g. Isaiah 37.31 − 2; Jeremiah 23.3.
3. The blamelessness of Noah and God's covenant with him, Genesis 6.

4. Donatism: a fourth-century movement in Africa concerned to preserve the purity of the Church by excluding those who, having weakened and apostasized under persecution, were repentant and wished for reinstatement.

5. Jansenism: after Jansen, seventeenth-century Bishop of Ypres. Five of his propositions for an excessively harsh and rigid form of religious life, deriving from the theology of St Augustine, were condemned in 1653.

6. J. A. T. Robinson *Honest to God,* SCM 1963.

7. From 1984, when Dr Jenkins was nominated to the See of Durham.

8. See, for example, *The Church and the Bomb,* Report of the General Synod Board of Social Responsibility 1982; *Miners' Strike 1984/85* (the call of church leaders for a negotiated settlement), February 1985, and the comments of individual bishops, e.g. the Archbishop of York, in January 1985.

9. 1986.

10. 'Put into': psychological mechanism known as *projective identification;* See ch. 3, pp. 63 — 4.

11. Positively, in the mobilizing of giving to such charities as *Children in Need* and *Live Aid* beyond any scale that could have been expected — *all* the need is put onto/into the recipients, and therefore the giving part of us is mobilized to an almost incredible degree; negatively, as in the very extreme polarizations at football matches resulting in war-like violence.

12. Throughout the OT, but focused in Leviticus.

13. For the task of apostleship see Romans 1.1 — 6.

14. See Jeremiah 26.12ff. for instance.

15. See King David's ministry in 1 Chronicles 16.

16. Church of England Articles of Religion, Article 26 (Book of Common Prayer); earlier formulation by St Augustine of Hippo during the Donatist controversy, Ep. 61.2.

17. John 13.34.

18. Psalm 139. 7 — 12.

19. 2 Samuel 11, 12.

20. 1 Kings 19.

21. e.g. 2 Corinthians 10, 11.

22. Luke 22.48.

23. John 4.6.

24. Mark 11.11 — 18.

25. Mark 15.34.

26. When gripped by a vision of devils attacking a dead man's body at a funeral; see *Complete Works of St Teresa* vol. 1, ed. and trs. E. Allison Peers, Sheed and Ward 1957.

27. When describing her raptures and visions and physical sufferings.

28. See, for example, *Seven Storey Mountain*, Sheldon Press 1978.

29. Romans 3.23.

30. Romans 7.20.

31. J. V. Taylor *The Go-Between God,* SCM 1972, p. 51.

THREE

Untying the Human Bundle

I suggested that we urgently need an understanding of how we come, humanly speaking, to be as we are; how we develop and grow from helpless babies into adults who take their place in the world as ministers (and other things too, of course, but it is ministers we are considering).

For me to attempt to communicate understanding is easier said than done. I cannot give a complete or even full account of human development for that would double the length of this book. Furthermore, there is more than one theory as to how development happens, and some ideas are in conflict with others. So what I am about to offer has at least two limitations. First, it is going to be focused rather than complete, as I need to address the question of why it is so difficult for us to relieve the pressures and stress under which we live.

Secondly, my approach is not going to be tied to the particular detail and superstructure of any *one* psycho-dynamic theory of development.[1] Some may say that this is an avoidance, that I should come out and take my stand on the theory that I most favour, and for which I can see most evidence. But this would, I feel, become tendentious and detract from the points I really want to make — which arise from the common aspect of various theories rather than from their differences.

It is not my intent that this chapter ultimately comes to read a bit like a textbook, as textbooks tend to be boring. Nevertheless, since the majority of readers may be more familiar with religious ideas than with psychological terms and language, I need to set things out from scratch in a way that may feel a bit textbookish. I cannot see any way to avoid this, and it is not for its own sake, but in order that we may allow the two disciplines to begin to overlap and enter into dialogue with each other.

We can 'read' our human dilemma rather like this: If we start from where we are, with our present everyday activity and attitudes, then we find that we seem to want to exercise value judgements not only upon our *actions* but also on our *feelings and experiences.*

Let us take two examples which are quite common in religious, or at least Christian, circles: 'I don't think I or other people should get or feel angry', and, 'I think self-denial is at the heart of the gospel'. We might dare to ask 'Why' to each of these. The answer may well come back, 'Anger causes broken relationships, murders, wars; lack of self-denial becomes selfishness, not caring for others, greediness and the rest'. Other possibilities do not get a look in, namely that when people get angry (at injustice or oppression, for instance) they often also mobilize energy to get things changed, or that there may be room in the scheme of things for us to be ourselves and feel and say what we want without necessarily making it impossible for other people to do the same. If we go back to Anne of our case studies: Could she not have negotiated with her community about staying *sometimes* after school so that she could participate more in school and they could see more of her?

The origin of such value judgements often seems to us to lie in the group or profession to which we belong. For instance the Church's official teaching is that we should not have sexual feelings, let alone act upon them, towards someone to whom we are not married. But in fact the corporate *and personal* aspects of such issues tend to be interwoven, and I believe that this is not accidental. Though we need to try to make a distinction between those feelings, prohibitions and experiences that are shared among people and groups and those which appertain more closely to the personal life of an individual, it is precisely factors in an individual's personal history and experience that may incline him or her towards participation in and identification with a particular group or milieu. That group will have, in turn, its own history and acquired stereotypes and myths regarding its own and other people's being and life, and inevitably these two processes,

Clergy Stress

that of the group or institution and that of the individual, will interact, to the probable amplification of each.

These processes may cause no trouble nor make for any sense of subjective stress and anxiety, for everyone in the system may be emotionally comfortable. People have chosen to be where their values match and fit, and indeed why should there, then, not be a straightforward progression and development of these values?

Unfortunately our experience shows that it doesn't quite work like that! Within the religious system controversies and scandals appear; people suddenly or gradually feel or act at variance with their stated values or creeds, and fears appear at the seams or even at the centre. Clearly we need to have an understanding of human nature which can give us insight into why we cannot and do not always feel and act the way our respectable self would like to. Some of what follows has already emerged but rather piecemeal; I want now to try to re-present it more coherently.

First, that which we observe, or indeed experience, of ourselves and other people is but the tip of the iceberg. There exists a more irrational, often less 'good' and less 'respectable' area of ourselves of which we are not easily aware. We have already seen hints of this in the section that looked at what the world can do to the Church and vice versa.[2] In other words, we have an unconscious as well as a conscious area of our being. We are a bigger bundle than we thought we were!

Second, I believe that the reason, at least in part, why we may stay unconscious of whole parts of ourselves is that these areas are painful, anxiety-provoking and even threatening to us. This is likely to be because they include impulses, desires and feelings that we think we ought not to be having, *and/or* because they evoke very painful experiences that we have already had at some point of our lives. If we let ourselves know and feel them they might arouse intolerable anxieties such that we might feel our very being and survival to be threatened. So we *defend* ourselves against remembering and knowing these areas in various sorts of ways, and we gravitate for support in this process towards membership of a group of people who use rather similar ways of 'forgetting', or who may have, in their personal or corporate histories similar experiences and desires which need to be forgotten.

Third, I am committed to the belief that the experiences and desires that have had to be 'forgotten', or kept out of consciousness are most likely to belong to our earlier rather than later experiences, that is, to childhood, when it would have been difficult to come to terms with or even make sense of them. This is not invariable — as shown when adults cannot come to terms with recent events such as accidents or bereavement, but even then it often emerges that this is based on earlier patterns of experience and survival. In early infancy we are very dependent and helpless and so in reality very vulnerable. We cannot talk, so we feel and sense often through our bodies. We cannot *say,* for instance, 'I am a bundle of fear, rage and hunger'. We can only feel it and suffer it, and with it, terrible anxieties such as being left in this state for ever, or being blown apart by the intensity of our sensations. Later on in childhood we *can* talk, but not always communicate with, the 'big' people around, and so are still often trapped in our feelings.

These last sentences may seem 'overdone'; indeed the intensity and primary importance of childhood experience is by no means universally accepted and is difficult to prove. There have been studies on this thesis, but it has not proved easy to apply the usual principles of research design to such material. Qualitative work on clinical case histories, such as Anna Freud and Melanie Klein's work on the analysis of children, supports it,[3] but I would be claiming more than is possible if I presented it as proven.

I do not want to say much more at this point about the sorts of feelings, experiences and desires that we need or want to forget; these will, I hope, emerge as we go along. But I do want, now, to expand on some of the *defences* we use to ward off our anxiety and achieve this 'forgetting'.

Forgetting

First, we can simply choose to forget that which we do actually know about. This action belongs to our conscious, even if not exactly rational, selves; if indeed we stop to think then we realize that it is likely to become a mug's game!

Things we are trying desperately to forget have an uncanny way of rising up and hitting us in the midriff when we least expect them to. If we have a motor accident we may be perfectly aware that we had it and want to forget its horror, but unfortunately there are far too many cars on the road plus the possibility of witnessing further and similar accidents for this to be a realistic and effective strategy. Similarly, the bereaved person who is consciously suffering from the sense of loss cannot be made safe from the invasion and 'knock-on' effect of other people's deaths and funerals, or from the difficult feelings aroused by proximity to other people's relationships. Straight forgetting is a rather precarious defence, even though people advocate it: 'Just try to forget all about it'. Elizabeth's boss suggested it, in effect, when she went to him for help, and it certainly did not work very well then.

If forgetting is likely to let us down, what are we to do? One of the possibilities is to turn further into ourselves, to more involuntary defence mechanisms, 'learnt' years ago in childhood when our anxieties were high and our strategies for external action limited. Such mechanisms have been given names such as 'repression', 'reaction formation', rationalization', 'avoidance', 'psychosomatic reaction', 'denial', and 'sublimation'.[4] In order to begin to understand and explore them I invite you into this imaginary scene.

Seven small boys, Alex, Bob, Charlie, David, Ernest, Fred and George are walking across a field. Suddenly Fred glimpses something some distance away, and he calls out to the others: 'Watch out, there's a bull down there, and it's charging.' They all react, but differently.

For our purposes I want us to assume two things, since we are allowed to construct an imaginary scene any way we like. First, nobody *consciously* lies in what they say or about their feelings. Second, there is, in fact, a deep wide ditch, hidden in a dip of the field, between the boys and the bull, and it can't be seen from where they are. So, the situation is not really dangerous, but there is no way they can know this.

Alex, Bob, Charlie and David all decide to 'get the hell out of here'. They turn tail and run back to the gate they came in by, climb, or rather fall, over it, arrive panting on the other side, and begin, rather sheepishly, to eye and talk to each other.

Alex is plainly terrified and in a panic; you can see it in his face and he is shaking all over and looking very pale. He says it's the worst fright he's ever had. Inside he vows never again to walk through a field with cows in it. At all costs he is going to *avoid* a repetition of this awful experience. The trouble is that if he carries this through systematically he could extend this to all fields and even the whole countryside, just in case cows should be around, one of which might just turn out to be a bull . . . life could become rather restricted, but anything would be better than that sort of fear.

Avoidance is a defence we probably all tend to use, for none of us likes awful, frightening situations, and, on one level, why should we put ourselves through them? But avoidance carried to extremes, when we generalize beyond the actual situation that produced the first experience, is a diminishing of our being. As a diminishing it is not quite a mental mechanism for it involves action, but the rationale we give ourselves for it is. In Alex's case the mechanism seems relatively obvious and is conscious: 'Bulls are frightening . . . I have just met a bull, and I don't want to do that again'. And in fact bulls *are* dangerous; the fear has some substance to it and to run is a useful defence. The defence gets out of hand, though, if we find we have to avoid all potentially similar situations.

But what about a fear of, and determination to avoid, things like supermarkets or tunnels? This seems irrational for there is nothing inherently frightening about either. It looks as if we have a much more complicated mechanism here, with the supermarket or tunnel 'standing for' something else — and we shall explore this when we return to Elizabeth's story in the next chapter.[5] The general point I am wanting to make here is that *avoiding action* is often a defence against *feelings.* Robert (of our stories) was displaying it when he didn't want to go on in-service courses; so was John when he dodged both his parishioners and his resentful feelings about them.

Bob also *looks* very frightened, but has another way of dealing with his fear. He proclaims to all and sundry: 'I suppose we could have stayed and seen what it would do, but I've always read that it's better to run. Also, look over there; there's a big, black cloud, and it's going to rain. Thank goodness the bull started us back and stopped us getting wet.' He *rationalizes,* that is, he sets his fear in a context so that its really fearful, out-of-control, elements get overlaid by more rational and sensible considerations.

As human beings with reasoning capacity, this way of keeping our feelings within bounds that we can tolerate becomes increasingly available to us. The point about *rationalization* is that it makes use of reality; it *is* better to get out of the way of a bull, and there's no point in getting soaked. But this reaction does divert us both from identifying the source of our feelings, and from feeling their full strength. We see it in the way we might talk after being turned down for a job. Saying something like 'on overall consideration I realized it wasn't the right job for me' can defend us against the full impact of the sense of disappointment and rejection.

Charlie and David do not look nearly as frightened as the other two. In fact they are not showing much at all, but are just aroused and panting from the exertion of running. This is borne out by what they say.

Charlie doesn't actually *say* much. As he rests, everything goes back to normal, heart, breathing and the rest, and he virtually 'drops' the incident for himself, though continuing to pay some attention to the others. All he does is to wonder aloud how a bull can be loose in a field without a notice to say so. But when he gets home that evening he has a violent tummy upset. He puts it down to his supper, rather unconvincingly, since he's eaten the same thing many times before with no ill effects. We could suggest instead that he is reacting *psychosomatically* to his frightening experience with the bull. Somehow he managed to resist and defend against feelings of fear by channelling them all into his body.

Putting it this way sounds as if Charlie 'decided' what to do and how to do it, but this is far from the case. People who react psychosomatically, of whom John of our stories is a prime example, do not decide to do so with the rational adult part of themselves. The process is involuntary and unconscious, as if our inner being somehow 'knows' that this is the only way to contain and dissipate unbearable feelings. The problem with this as a defence is that it is very unhelpful and can even be dangerous or life-threatening to us. It cuts us off from our feelings and so impoverishes us, and the resulting illnesses are often far more serious than a tummy upset.

Suppression of our feelings in this way is thought to contribute to asthma, migraine, colitis and even heart disease and cancer, and these possibilities are clearly no joke.

David, like Charlie, arrives back at the gate without any obvious signs of fear. He also doesn't say very much because, for him, there genuinely seems not much to say. There was a bull in the field, bulls can be dangerous and the obvious thing to do is to get out of their way. But he doesn't feel frightened. He does take a moment to wonder how it is that the others are frightened, but then dismisses this. The question we can ask is how much he is *repressing* his fear down below his conscious awareness. *Repression* is the name given to the psychological defence whereby feelings (and desires) really do not seem to be there for us. We truly believe we do not have them, or it may not even occur to us to ask that question.

It may be that the feelings we think we are not having could relate to experiences we have had in the past, or they could belong to another part of ourselves that we would prefer not to see the light of day because it has seemed/would seem disreputable or unacceptable either to ourselves or others. We get hints of our repressed feelings or selves in dreams or in the sudden moments when we react in very uncharacteristic ways. Sometimes somebody else's experience or behaviour, gross anger for example, triggers a hitherto unknown extreme reaction of our own. Or we can have in our adult life an experience like bereavement that is rather similar, in the feelings it produces, to some other loss or disaster in our earlier life which we have pushed away from us because it is too painful to think about.

In all this we have temporarily lost sight of Ernest, Fred and George, but they are very much still with us, still in the field for they do not join the headlong rush to the gate. Ernest and Fred prepare for action, taking off their jackets and being prepared to throw these in the path of the oncoming bull. George does virtually nothing but stick around.

Ernest and Fred take the same action, but their feelings are different. Ernest, like David, does not seem frightened. If we had met him before we would know that he thinks fear is sissy and he tries very hard not to react fearfully to any event that overtakes him. In actual fact this does not seem very hard to him because he does not really experience fear. We can ask the same question of him as of David as to how much he is *repressing* his fear, but there is something added in his case. He seems to have formed what is called a *reaction formation* against fear. It is sissy, and you either don't feel it or don't act as if you did.

Reaction formation happens when we not only repress a feeling but strive consciously always to do and feel its opposite. Religious people sometimes seem to behave in this sort of way towards 'unrespectable' feelings such as doubt, depression, anger . . . the list could go on but may differ a bit according to whether we belong to the Jewish or Christian tradition.

The difficulty with both *repression* and *reaction formation,* is that keeping them up — that is, keeping other unconscious feelings battened-down — 'locks up' both whole parts of ourselves and a lot of emotional energy so that they are not available to our conscious life, thus impoverishing our being.

Fred, unlike Ernest, *is* frightened and later says so. He explains: 'Yes, I was terrified and everything was pounding inside me. But I know what you're supposed to do with bulls, and since I'm the tallest and have the longest legs I thought I'd have the best chance of diverting him and being able to get away afterwards. In fact being so frightened almost helped as I felt I could run faster than I ever had.' Fred is attempting to *sublimate* his fear; he knows he has it but he is trying to subdue it and even use it in the service of something more important — covering the retreat of his friends.

In one sense *sublimation* is not a defence in the ways that the other reactions are, because it does not operate by pushing away feelings and desires; but the alternative use that is made of them does take off from the feelings themselves. Religious, or priests vowed to celibacy, have to try to sublimate their sexual desires and feelings, and use that part of themselves in another way. The problem is that it is sometimes very difficult for us not to kid ourselves and think we are sublimating a part of our being when in fact we may be avoiding, rationalizing, or repressing.

We are left with George. George doesn't run; afterwards he *denies* that he felt frightened either. This looks like repression, except for the rest of what he says. He says: 'I wasn't scared — the bull wouldn't have harmed us anyway [but remember that the ditch in the field is hidden from him]; they don't really charge at people.' What he has done, as his basis for not feeling frightened, is to distort reality; for it actually *is* the case that bulls are dangerous.

It is possible for us to *deny* feelings and experience even when this seems to be at gross variance with reality as we and other people would normally interpret it. This denial is different from merely *choosing* to forget for it tends to be unconscious. We actually do not know that this is what we are doing; for a moment at least George really believed that bulls were not dangerous. I have come across it in people's memories of the war days when the horror of separated families and uncertain future really seem to have gone out of awareness: 'it wasn't really so bad', or, 'I never really feared we'd be invaded or bombed' — when other people also there at the time remember something quite different. We can see this tendency in the over-nice minister who says, 'I never feel angry, and I don't think I have ever done so in my life', or in the person who says, 'I never feel depressed' and goes on to cite the gospel as a good reason for not doing so.

Probably we all *deny* at some point or other. For example, most of us deny the possibility of a nuclear holocaust, even though we know it could happen. If we did not do so it would make daily life very unpleasant and threatening. But it is a defence we tend to have to use against extreme threat, and people who use it a lot of the time, especially when people around them see no need for it, are in fact saying that their underlying feelings and sense of threat are so powerful that anything goes in order that they shall not be felt — even the distortion of reality. One example is when people cannot face the loss of bereavement and live as if the other person was still there, keeping their room, clothes and other belongings exactly as they were. When that happens we think that the person is ill and disturbed, and sustained denial does indicate disturbance of a deep kind.

I hope that this example of seven small boys and their different reactions to threat gives us a sense of some of the ways in which we defend ourselves. I have not addressed the questions of how we learn them, and how we acquire individual, habitual and favourite defences. These questions are very complicated to explore, but my contention is that we learned them in childhood when we felt anxious, threatened and relatively powerless. The different defences we use do, I think, reflect the stages of our life at which the threat appeared.

To react psychosomatically implies a threat early in our life when we lacked the power of self-expression, as does the use of *denial* which suggests a helplessness in the face of reality so great that reality itself has to be distorted. We are at our most helpless when we are most young. Paradoxically, we can also, as babies, fantasize, at least for periods, that we are omnipotent. Food, rest and a person are 'on tap' for us; better to believe, erroneously, that we can always command them than to face the helpless feelings of actually being without them.

On the other hand, *rationalization* and *avoidance* seem to emanate from later periods when we had more organized mental capacities and more possibilities for taking evasive action.

Apart from these involuntary and unconscious sorts of 'forgetting' there are a number of ways of defending ourselves which depend on other mechanisms associated with a process of dividing up our experience of ourselves and usually using other people to help us in this. These defences have also been given names: we talk of 'splitting', 'stereotyping', 'scape-goating' and 'projection'.[6] To explore them I would like, once again, to use the medium of a story, but this time one that is already known to most, if not all, of us; the fairy story usually known as *Beauty and the Beast*.[7]

This story has several versions, but in the one I am using Beauty is the beautiful, kind, compassionate, favourite daughter of a rich merchant. Her two elder sisters are spiteful, capricious and selfish. In the course of a journey their father promises to bring them each a present. Beauty asks only for a rose whilst the others ask for expensive gifts. Misfortune overtakes the merchant; he is saved by finding a mysterious house where he and his horse, both starving, are cared for by an unseen hand. It is when he plucks a rose from the garden before leaving that the owner reveals himself as a terrible Beast who exacts as punishment for the theft of the rose the promise that its recipient shall come and live with him. The story goes on: Beauty characteristically accepts the charge; she lives with the Beast but rebuffs his love because of his repulsive ugliness. He lets her return home once to see her sad and ageing father, but warns her that if she does not return to him in three days he will die. The sisters, equally characteristically, try to prevent Beauty from fulfilling her promise and when she does return the Beast is dying. It is only by her loving kiss, hitherto withheld from him, that he is saved *and* is transformed into the prince that he had been before being put under a spell by a wicked fairy. They are then free to live happily ever after. Magic runs right through the tale with miraculous transportations across time and space.

This is a very shortened version and does violence to the original, for which I apologise, but I have used it because I think it illustrates so well some of the difficult ideas I am wanting to set out.

The first point comes from the title itself. Beauty and the Beast are opposites. Beauty is beautiful and the Beast is ugly and repulsive. There are other extremes too: Beauty is all good and her sisters are all bad. It is as if beauty and ugliness, good and bad have been *split apart — and* kept apart. The Beast can have no intrinsic beauty and Beauty herself keeps it this way; she cannot embrace him and his ugliness.

We have already come across the idea of *splitting* in Chapter 2. Recapitulating, one group of people can be all good and another all bad; God can be seen as all-loving and the Devil as all-punishing; religious people can be all-caring and non-religious people not caring at all. Or we can see ourselves as all-hurt and another person as all-hurting, or ourselves as all-considerate and another as all-neglectful. In this tendency to use the word 'all' — *all*-caring, *all*-hurtful — we can identify two further processes which help us intensify and preserve this splitting. We can *idealize* that which we want to keep 'good' with no badness in it. Or we can *denigrate* that which we want to keep 'bad' with no goodness in it. In the story Beauty comes over as too good to be true; her near-cruelty in persistently rejecting the Beast's love passes unmarked. On the other hand, her sisters have no redeeming features; they are portrayed as unequivocally bad, and no chinks are allowed in this.

There is another way, too, in which we can split and divide up people and groups of people, known as *stereotyping*. This happens when we consciously *and* unconsciously invest a group of people with attributes and characteristics that they may not in fact possess, either as individuals or as a group. Sometimes we improve on this by giving the groups labels — often derogatory — such as 'wogs' or 'queers'. In the religious context there is still some strange stereotyping of Catholics by Anglicans, of Low Church by High Church, and vice versa. Furthermore our labelling and categorizing persists because we take care that we do not test it out by relating to one of the group concerned.

This stereotyping process is also illustrated by the story. We have a stereotype of Beasts as ugly and repulsive; Beauty will not get near enough to him, will not embrace him to find out otherwise. When she finally does manage to do so the Beast, in the story, is magically transformed. But if we take it this way we miss the point that he had *always* been the Prince. We can, if we will, see the loosing of the spell by the embrace not as a transformation of the Beast but as a transformation of Beauty's *perception of him.*

Stereotyping is an excellent way of defending ourselves from having to change our views about another group of people. Unfortunately it keeps the groups very split apart and prevents one learning anything valuable that the other might have to teach. It can also become something far worse: *scapegoating.* When we do this we first stereotype and then attack, as has happened to despised minorities in and outside the communities of religion. The strength of the attack seems to be commensurate with our need to keep the split going, for perhaps we fear that otherwise we would be overwhelmed and overrun by this despised other.

It is obviously difficult for us to give up our split perception even when someone tries to get us to check it against actual experience. The Beast almost has to die before Beauty can embrace him. We maintain our splitting as if our lives depended on it. And indeed at the time when we first had need of it we may well have felt that it really did. For *splitting* is thought to be a defence originating from a very early period in our lives when we needed to separate and protect our good, life-giving feelings from the intensity of the 'bad', destructive feelings arising in us through the inevitable frustration and helplessness of babyhood.

But if these 'bad' feelings are there and are not 'allowed' to be a part of us, what on earth are we supposed to do with them? We have to have recourse to yet another process known as *projection.*

Is Beauty *really* all-good and all-beautiful and are her sisters *really* without any good parts to them at all? *In the story* it is the sisters who make it impossible for her to go back to the Beast when once she has been allowed away, even though he will die if she does not. They steal the charm which will 'magic' her back. Since it is a fairy story and *all* is magic we, perhaps, are allowed to do 'magic' with the story and write it another way. Suppose, instead of it being the sisters' fault we could allow ourselves to think that maybe Beauty herself is reluctant and wants not to be able to go back, but cannot admit this feeling to herself since it does not square up with her being kind and good. Could she not have put out from herself, that is *projected,* that desire on to her sisters? Is their supposed action really her own wish 'out there'? Yet it is only when she can go back and embrace the Beast (her own Beastliness?) that transformation can take place.

Most of us must be familiar with the sense of 'I really dislike so and so; the way he or she is, thinks or acts gets my goat.' The more violent our objection the more salutary it might be for us to see if there is anything of that detested quality in ourselves. It may be that there is and we dislike it so much and cannot accept it that we split it off and then 'project' it out from us and only observe it in another person. Sometimes we about-turn on this, as when we see another person as everything we've wanted to be and feel we aren't. So 'good' qualities can also get projected away from ourselves as, for example, in the congregation who see their minister as all-understanding and all-caring and themselves as inadequate and sinful.

There is an extension of this form of defence which is more powerful than just putting something *on to* another person and it happens when we are really desperate. If, for example, we have a very strong unconscious need not to feel the emotion of anger — maybe we fear at some level of our being that it could tear us apart — it may not be enough just to look at another person and see them as furious or whatever. We can, quite unconsciously, try to put our unacknowledged anger into the other person and get him or her to behave angrily *towards us*. We may then come to feel attacked and persecuted by something we see as *outside* us which in fact originated *inside* us. The name given to this sort of process is *projective identification*.

The person responding to us sometimes actually feels what we need them to feel and then does react accordingly; when this happens we call it *introjective identification*. If their reaction is very unlike how they usually feel or act they may be able to twig that something odd is happening and begin to resolve it. If it is rather nearer the bone for them then the situation may go on escalating unchecked.

To use the defence of projection effectively and devastatingly generally requires the selection, without necessarily being aware of this, of a target person who has, in the depth of their being and unknown to them, something that more or less fits the projected emotion — a sort of 'hook' on which rather heavy things can then be hung.

The possibility of this sort of process going on may help us to understand such phenomena as the inflammation of mob violence already cited in Chapter 2,[8] or the sudden appearance in a congregation of the very vices that the minister may spend a lot of his sermon time denouncing. These clear-cut examples are, though, rather extreme. Most often and most complicatedly there is a mixture of projection and reality, and it is hard for us to sort out the difference.

Some of the ways of 'forgetting' and defending ourselves are obviously more crude and primitive than others. To divide everything into black and white or to say that something is not in us but only in another person is quite drastic and is usually undertaken with a considerable degree of unconsciousness. The more primitive methods — denial, splitting and projection — stem from our earlier childhood periods when our helplessness was greatest and our need for drastic action correspondingly great. At the same time they are potentially dangerous and even destructive because they depend on a distortion of current reality. They usually have to be employed when the feelings that we would otherwise have to face in ourselves are also powerful, primitive and even violent, such as sexuality, envy, anger, hate and murderousness.

The sorts of situation in which these strong feelings and defences emerge are clearly likely to be those which reproduce something of our primitive nature and surroundings. Isabel Menzies, in a study of nurses in the NHS,[9] found that nurses needed these defences a lot perhaps just because they had to work constantly near the fringes of life, in caring for helpless people in their most primitive and fundamental bodily functions, and with the issues of life and death.

It does not seem to me too fanciful to suggest that the Church, as an institution, is subject to rather similar pressures. Religion and church life deal, too, with issues of life and death, as well as eternity and non-being. Of course religion has its own more sophisticated language and rituals which parallel the routine and rituals of hospital, but the undertones of dependence, feeding, maternal care, paternal love and punishment are all there. Religion deals with primitive material, and so we may find ourselves caught in primitive conflicts and anxieties and using the most powerful of defence mechanisms. This may give us a clue as to why the debates that take place within religious bodies can become so entrenched, so painful and even violent. Fundamentalism, for example, is about the basic question of who is included in the love of God. The Jewish/Christian divide could represent, on one level, two rivals for the same father. The ordination of women goes deeply into the relationship between men and women, and debates about belief and the nature of God can touch deeper anxieties about being held in security or left in a void.

In these sorts of religious debates anger is usually generated along with some quite violent behaviour. Since these themselves would often be 'taboo' in religious circles the defence of *denial* — 'it's not anger, it's righteous indignation', — or the defence of *projection* — 'it's the other people who are behaving lawlessly and destructively; we only act according to our conscience' — tend to operate. Tragically much of this remains hidden from all concerned, so it is hard to arrive at any real resolution.

As individual people and as ministers we all get caught up in religious and other more personal conflicts, and we all need some defences. We need some armour against being overtaken by all our deepest feelings and desires at once. Otherwise, if we experienced them in their full intensity all the time, we could be overwhelmed.

Most of us achieve some sort of equilibrium in ourselves, but the nature of that equilibrium will vary depending on the relative strength and imperturbability of the defences that we produce from within ourselves, and the strength of the pressures from the environment outside and around us. For instance, we can have a defence against feeling jealousy that is strong enough, and does indeed prevent us from feeling that rather unpleasant emotion, unless a situation arises — as it did for Elizabeth of our case histories — that really triggers the emotion. In this sort of moment defences which had seemed strong enough sometimes collapse and the person has to face the emotion. This can, and often does, feel devastating, and the more the particular feeling has been pushed away, the more devastating it feels.

I am not implying that all defence against our feelings and impulses is unproductive. Some of the most effective caring work has been done by people such as Mother Teresa of Calcutta or by ministers who seem to defy all the laws of nature and/or physical and emotional health by working in the most appalling conditions and by offering and giving a total availability without, apparently, any twinges of resentment or doubt as to the conviction that this is what they were made for. I am not claiming, either, that this ability comes, necessarily, from impenetrable personal defences; it can represent a choice and sacrifice made in awareness and fully lived out. Some people can do what the rest of us cannot and it would be a carping attitude to leap to psychology and suggest that this automatically means that they are unhealthily defending against something in themselves. That would smack of envy and a sort of psychological one-upmanship. Their defence may be that of *sublimation* which depends on a quite mature integration of conscious and unconscious. Nevertheless, I do believe that *most* of us need to function less totally and our level of anxiety fluctuates more. Our equilibrium is, therefore, potentially vulnerable to disturbance. It is the disturbing of a present state of equilibrium that is one of the factors underlying manifest stress, and it seems to me that it happens in three ways.

First, people's habitual defences may be breached, often by an unexpected happening or life event. This makes them experience forgotten and sometimes forbidden feelings in ways that feel very threatening.

Second, the way of defending against impulses and feelings can itself become exhausting and debilitating if it has to be kept up unremittingly.

Third, we may ourselves embark on a process of relaxing some of our more rigid and constrictive ways of defending ourselves. We may 'decide' on some level that we no longer need them and may then get in touch with more of our unconscious. In this way we can decide that we do not need or do not want to wear, in or out of church, anything that proclaims us to be ministers and which seems to cut us off from being an 'ordinary' human being. Or we can feel that we cannot and do not want to meet people's expectations of availability, tolerance and the rest. We are somehow compelled to experience and explore the less compliant, less 'good' part of ourselves.

The question of whether we *can* and *should* violate others' expectations in this way is one we shall need to return to later. What can be said now is that we are very likely to experience conscious and powerful conflict with our group or institution if it is not moving in the same direction. The reverse is sometimes true: an institution changes and the individual cannot or does not want to change with it. Either way, this conflict between individual and institution causes stress, although what is uncomfortable for one person is not necessarily so for another. For example, some ministers have felt very strained by apparent 'blocking' movements in the Church of England on such issues as marriage reform and the ordination of women. Others, differently made, have felt equally stressed when required to function in a post-Vatican Council Roman Catholic Church, just because they feel threatened by the widespread reforms.

So, conditions arise which disturb our usual equilibrium.

What happens to us if this disturbance is for us excessively anxiety-provoking, or threatens to become so? It is then that we tend to forsake our emotional 'language' and resort to that of action or symptom.

We can try to restore equilibrium by resorting either to more primitive and powerful psychological mechanisms or to what are essentially other kinds of defence, for example, compulsive overwork. Or we can allow the emergence of habits which are probably themselves going to be unhelpful and destructive to us. Of these, addiction to alcohol, smoking and promiscuous sexuality are three examples. Some of these strategies are more acceptable than others in religious circles, and therefore likely to be longer lasting. It is usually 'OK' to overwork, and 'not OK' to become an alcoholic. So the latter, if it happens, is likely to be noticed and queried far quicker than the former — but both, if unchecked, lead to eventual breakdown of one sort or another.

Alternatively, our being may not lead us into these sorts of habits, but more directly into symptoms. These can be either of the body or, more explicitly, of the emotions. If mild and not too inconveniencing they effectively do the trick in lowering anxiety and restoring us to some sort of equilibrium. A mild tendency to stomach-ache after an exhausting and fraught meeting can give us an excuse for avoiding such meetings in the future. Vague depression can be lived with, especially if it can be interpreted as something spiritual.

The very mildness of some conditions is in a way tragic, just because it can be lived with for ever. People can come to accept firing on three cylinders, without ever realizing their potential. If the trouble becomes acute then we are forced to do something about it. In the short term this is often more painful, but in the long term it can be more beneficial. Four of the people in our case histories come into the second category; their breakdown of equilibrium is not mild and they are aware of needing help. Robert comes into the first category, and we cannot know whether he will ever want to explore himself more; we are not given the end of his story.

That these people have got into a muddle is clear; what is not so clear is *how* they got into this muddle and what conflicts, obvious and more hidden, are operating for them. In the next chapter I want to return more specifically to their stories and to attempt to explore and identify some of the conflicts that underlie their unhappiness and their symptoms, using among other things some of the ideas and concepts that have emerged from this present chapter.

Before I do this there is one point I need to stress. I was very exercised as to whether to *separate* the material in these last two chapters and give the human, psychological dimension a chapter to itself, for the aim of this book is to try *not* to split the religious and the human but to let them interact with each other. For clarity's sake I found I had to make the separation, but in what follows I want to facilitate their coming together again. I have also come to realize, as the work unfolds, that I am writing to a sort of *spiral* design, introducing ideas and images, and, at this first point of meeting, only taking them so far. Later on they re-emerge, and hopefully the whole goes deeper. This process has to me come to seem inevitable since we are working towards a deeper engagement of the two disciplines and a deeper understanding of people caught up in them.

Notes

1. For a helpful introduction to and summary of the major psychodynamic thinkers see: D. Brown and J. Pedder *Introduction to Psychotherapy,* Part 1, 'Psychodynamic Principles', Tavistock Publications 1979, or N. Symington *The Analytic Experience,* Free Association Books 1986.
2. See ch. 2; 'The minister in relation to the wider community', p. 40ff.
3. See A. Freud *The Ego and the Mechanisms of Defence,* English tr. Hogarth Press and Institute of Psychoanalysis 1937; see Juliet Mitchell, ed. *The Selected Melanie Klein,* Penguin 1986, chs. 1 and 2.
4. A. Freud, op. cit., and a summary of defence mechanisms can be found in D. Brown and J. Pedder, op. cit., pp. 25−33.
5. See ch. 4 p. 81ff., but especially p. 83.
6. See note 4.
7. Madame de Villeneuve in *Les Contes Marins* (1740−1); this version from Philippa Pearce *Beauty and the Beast,* Longman Young 1972.
8. See p. 43.
9. I. E. P. Menzies *Social Systems as a Defence against Anxiety,* Tavistock Institute of Human Relations 1970.

FOUR

The Story Starts to Unfold

What has gone wrong with the five people in our case histories? Are we in a better position to tease this out as a result of our explorations in Chapter 3? I want to consider them in turn and examine their unique and particular difficulties, both those that are obvious, and those which may underlie their distress. We can then use such common threads as may emerge to enable a more general reflection.

John

The first thing we notice about John is that strain has shown itself in his *body*. Then we see that to an extent this is always what has happened to him — he had a stomach ulcer when he was worried about his university exams, but, and perhaps most significantly, we notice that it was a feature of his childhood as well. We were told at the end of his story how much his mother fussed over his slightest ailment during schooldays, and even got the hint that this was the 'language' she most easily understood.

In most families there grows up a culture about distress and illness. In some families verbalizing emotional distress or showing feelings is not on, but being physically ill is, and becomes the best or even the only way to achieve attention or sometimes affection. In other families neither expressing feelings nor being ill seems really 'allowed', and there is then the considerable problem of the kettle or saucepan, so to speak, erupting when it has reached the point of nearly boiling over. I put the word 'allowed' in inverted commas because as written it looks at first as if families negotiate and agree consciously on these sorts of rules, which of course they do not. For one thing the results that emerge are often too nonsensical to have been intended or desired! They are arrived at unawares, are often unknown in the overt sense to anyone in the family, and may be the product of family tradition going back over more than one generation, or of the particular interactions and reactions that go on in the family over a period of time.

From his story we can hypothesize that John came from an 'illness is OK' family, or at least that was how his mother construed the position. His father seems not to have been very much on the scene, and this indeed may have been part of the problem. Where was his anxious mother to put her distress and that of her son, if her husband was not easily available to share it? We wonder at the relationships, overall, in this family, but the point that we are most interested in now is that John seems to be repeating a very long-standing pattern of expressing worry and disturbance in physical terms, and that he is in all probability unaware of this. He is like Charlie of the seven small boys with the bull; he is using the defence of *psychosomatic reaction* rather than being able to feel his true feelings. If he does not acquire some self-understanding in this area he could potentially put himself in the hands of the doctors for life. If this does not happen, or indeed even if it does, another likely result is that John will let himself do what, as we see from his story, part of him seems to want. He can become really careless, disillusioned and deeply embittered, possibly continuing to do just enough to get by with his parishioners and his hierarchy. It is not too hard to extend this picture into the rather frightening caricature of the thin, ill, humourless and loveless clergyman.

What really underlies his strain and makes him so uncomfortable that his health is becoming endangered? In many ways John's difficulties look very similar to those experienced by others who serve and care for people.

We wonder where his own support comes from, particularly since he lives alone: from friends, colleagues, superiors or from nowhere? We know from his background that as a child he did not get much help from his father who was so often away. This pattern is likely to militate against him being able to turn easily to senior colleagues; his very close relationship with his mother can go some way to explaining why he is

vulnerable to the overattentiveness of some of his female
parishioners, though I am not wanting to suggest simplisti-
cally that this is the whole story.

John obviously has a problem in taking time off, which
shows sometimes in wanting more free time and sometimes
in redoubled activity. There is a question, too, of how he
copes with failure; we have hints from his earlier story —
implied difficulties at school and at university — that this
has always been a problematic area for him. What, too, of the
problem of not being appreciated by those whom he serves?
Possible problems lie in becoming disconsolate and even
depressed, or in becoming angry and bitter with people and
their demands. He has to face, as do many in the caring
professions — particularly those working in deprived inner-
city areas — an environment in which there seems to be too
much irresolvable need, so it will be difficult to say, 'I have
done enough', or even, 'I have done a satisfactory job'.
Furthermore, these environmental stresses are *in reality*
irresolvable, at least for an individual. He or she can feel
worthless in himself or frustrated and angry with the social
and political system. But the end result is often a deeply
wearying sense of being caught and paralysed in a feeling of
helplessness and of not being able to change anything.

John is also, and in particular, a minister of religion and he
faces, therefore, additional pressures that his secular
colleagues most probably do not.

First, it is especially difficult for him to estimate and
achieve success for there could be so many criteria: increased
church attendance, increased maturity, spiritual growth and
responsibility among the laity, or a worthwhile contribution
to the well-being of the neighbourhood. The two latter are
exceedingly difficult to measure. It has emerged from work
on job satisfaction and associated well-being[1] that inability to
achieve results is a cause of dissatisfaction and stress. In
John's style of working stress becomes many-faceted, with
frustration and uncertainty being experienced in just too
many areas at once. Any one or two are containable, but in
work as diffuse and ambiguous as that of ministry the
additive factor can become intolerable.

Second, John is required to proclaim the gospel, to preach,
to teach in areas that usually belong to the 'private' life of a

professional. Furthermore it is apparently required of him that he should be, in the way he lives out his personal life, an exemplary model of the faith he teaches. So, for John, the separation or 'boundary' between professional and personal, in terms of time, space and emotions is complex and difficult to manage. Other 'carers' have more definite work hours, and, usually, a 'safe' distance between themselves and those they serve.

Third, John and those in similar positions are often seen as having an enviable degree of autonomy in their work, as compared to other professionals. But this very freedom can involve a blurring of the lines of accountability and responsibility, and so become, in itself, a source of strain.

The three factors above are quite overt and observable. But if we now look beneath the surface we can find other more hidden possibilities of stress. One of these is John's single state, which, in itself, is perfectly observable, but we are not told anything of why he is single and lives alone. It may be out of conviction stemming from his understanding of the nature of priesthood, or from lack of opportunity, or from a personal difficulty in making and sustaining close relationships. Alternatively it could be that his sexual orientation is such as to make marriage an impossibility. Perhaps John is well aware of why he remains single, perhaps not. In either case there may well be some inner conflict, and some ongoing stress in coping with other people's expectations.

There seem to be other things going on within John, probably not apparent to anyone else, which must be confusing for him. How is it that things that have been precious to him such as prayer and his belief have become an area of distress? Why is he oscillating between wanting too much time off and denying his need for any? And, lastly, what is going on between him and his congregation, that they expect so much and are sometimes so ungrateful? The last chapter inclines us to suspect *splitting and projection.*

From our detailed analysis of John's position we can begin to make some general points that we may find repeated when we look at the other case histories.

Clearly one issue is that of distinguishing and keeping clear the boundaries of personal and professional life. This is hard for all caring professionals but is, I think, made more difficult for ministers of religion just because they often live 'on the job' and their raw material is the whole of life and not just a part of it.

Then again, we can identify a conflict between personal integrity and expectation, whether the latter emanates from self or others. We see this most clearly in John's emerging doubts. How is he to be himself and let his inner being struggle and perhaps change *and* still keep on with the task of preaching and proclaiming in the way that people expect?

Thirdly, we see some glimpses of conflict between what we might call *duty* and *desire.* Of course no one can be entirely free of this; neither would it necessarily be desirable if we could. Yet in so far as religion seems to involve a quite considerable number of moral imperatives designed to achieve an ideal state of human functioning, conflicts of this nature may be more numerous and severe for religious people than for those without commitment to this kind of belief system. *A fortiori,* the most acute expression of such conflict is found sometimes in religion's representative and professional people, namely ministers.

This sort of conflict is often present in the sexual field, for here 'duty', as discerned and encountered through the life and teaching of the Church, can easily be at variance with the natural human desire for fulfilment. The conflict has perhaps intensified in recent years when the mores of society at large have changed and relaxed and the official teaching of the Church has not. Lay people may sometimes feel more free than ministers to engage with the religious tradition in such a way that it is in dialogue with the thinking of society, sometimes to the modification of both within an individual's lifestyle. The process is harder for ministers just because they are not private individuals, and the issue of their expectations of themselves is further complicated by other people's expectations of them. So, an ordinand or minister who divorces and wishes to remarry, or a minister whose sexual orientation is primarily homosexual[2] is under considerable pressure and stress. The source of this is partly internal, relating to his or her own understanding of the demands of vocation, and partly external, stemming from the way in which these demands are currently interpreted within the religious bodies.

For John there may indeed be a conflict between duty and desire in the sexual area, though we are not told enough about him to be sure of this. But there does seem to be some similar conflict going on with respect to his conscientiousness about work: his sense of duty impels him on, while his desire sometimes seems to be rampantly suggesting that he throws all to the winds and does exactly what he likes.

A much more difficult problem to identify may well be a hidden and unconscious conflict around the issue of *caring*: caring for others, and support and caring for self. We are made aware of this in John through the 'Yo-Yoing' he seems to be going through as to whether he wants to be available to his parishioners or not, and the strange and near-violent changes of mood he experiences in respect to them. Sometimes he feels almost 'hounded' by them, and indeed it is then that he 'cuts out' and his body bears the brunt of the disturbance. All this must be almost intolerably confusing for him in his role of a caring professional and a member of the group which, in its concern for people, is historically the prototype for all of the caring professions.

We have spent a lot of time with John and discovered some sources of conflict that are particular to him and his situation. Others, such as those involving integrity and expectation, duty and desire, personal and professional life are more general, and we are likely to find variations on these themes throughout ministry. So I would ask you to keep these ideas in mind as we turn now to look at the other four people.

Anne

Anne is in a very different external position from John. She looks as if she has a secure background in her community, so she can hardly suffer from the problems of lack of support and loneliness. Yet a reading of her story suggests that, *for her,* the support of her home community is more apparent than real; she cannot let anyone there know how she is feeling until she actually erupts. From what we are told of her early life we wonder if perhaps this has always been so. She was the eldest and had to look after her younger brothers and sisters. Perhaps the support of her parents was never easily available to her, but the memory of this has been forgotten, or more probably *repressed,* as being just too painful to keep in consciousness. Instead she now shows a difficulty in saying how she is feeling and in asking for help.

She has some obvious conflicts between duty and desire and between personal integrity and expectation, and these may be exacerbated by her being a Religious and so not really having any boundary between her personal and professional life. As a Religious, does she have any right to a 'private' life? We gather that she would like to spend more time at school to come to grips with the difficulties she is facing there, but feels that her duty is to be at home with her community. She feels in herself, at the heart of her being, that she is not coping very well, yet senses that the expectation is that she should cope, and keep her end up as a 'good' Religious. This expectation will no doubt seem to her to stem from the ideal of the religious life and the rule and constitution of her order, yet as we read her story again we can see that it may have its roots in much earlier and formative experience — namely her parents instilling into her that she should be a good Religious to justify the sacrifice she asked from the family in removing herself and her energies from them.

Maybe, too, she hasn't been able to allow, in herself, for the confusion that the changed life of her order could have induced. To go from habit to no-habit, from convent school to local comprehensive, from the more impersonal life of a large community to the intimate life of a small group, and all in a few years, is quite a tall order. Can she, or anybody, really be expected to make the transition completely smoothly? And, after all, she is not as young as some of the others in the house, and is likely to have adapted more thoroughly to the old regime.

Nothing in her early training really prepared her for the sort of personal relationship she is currently experiencing with the younger nun. In the past you didn't get close enough to other people for that sort of thing to happen, let alone get talked about. On one level she 'knows' it from her relationship with her younger sister at home, but that's another story and why should it occur to her to connect the two experiences, separated as they are by both time and the different 'worlds'?

She worries about how to understand and take better care of the children in her class whose problems are foreign to her, but she is clearly not good at taking care of herself. She knows she is exhausted and scrappy, but seems to find it impossible either to let up or to turn to anyone for help.

In Anne we can see a number of pointers to the interplay of the feelings and defences that I outlined in the last chapter. We have already noted that she has perhaps *repressed* her childhood experience of having to take care of others rather than be taken care of herself, but there are other pointers. First, why is she so shy with the men in the staffroom? Is it because they could stir up in her feelings to do with sexuality that she has never really experienced before? Entering her order at eighteen it may well be that she has never really been in touch with that part of herself, or that she has and has possibly had, unconsciously, to *deny* it in order to cope with the ideal of celibacy. We cannot be sure, but these are possibilities.

Second, she is experiencing quite a lot of anger which she seems to think is wrong and 'irreligious'. Worse still, when it comes to the sister in the community she senses that it could be quite a lot stronger than anger if she let it: hate, perhaps, and that of course is unthinkable.

How on earth is she to handle these feelings? It would be a lot more comfortable to stay not knowing too much about her sexuality — to keep it *repressed* and not causing too much pain and disturbance. To this end her unconscious may sense that it might not be such a good thing to learn and talk a lot more about the children's problems and those of their families; it might make it harder to keep all this area battened down, and so she *avoids* this opportunity. For we are told that she assumes, rather than knows, that her community would mind if she stayed at school a bit longer. Perhaps on some deep level, and unknown to her, it suits her not to ask them for fear that they might actually say yes. It looks as if Anne could be *projecting* onto her community her own uncertainties and ambivalence about staying at school.

Anne assumed also that her Superior would not notice or care that she is angry and upset; in part, there is some reality in this since she did not notice until the eruption happened. But then the query, 'Why didn't you tell me you were so depressed?' leaves us with the question of who doesn't want to know about Anne's feelings — Anne herself or her

Superior? It could be even more complicated if feelings from the past are coming in. Is Anne seeing the 'real' person of her Superior, or seeing in her the mother who never really had time for her in childhood, and so *projecting* into the Superior hostile and uncaring feelings with which she can then readily identify?

The *projecting* is not necessarily all being done by Anne. The other members of staff could, for their part, be *stereotyping* her as a nun, seeing her as detached, remote and unfriendly, and so making it more difficult for her to be otherwise. We cannot tell if this is so, but we can suspect that an element of it is present, *and* that Anne herself is possibly compounding this from her own stereotype of religious life which the externally-imposed reforms of Vatican II have not necessarily dispelled.

Yet, despite all this, Anne *is* feeling self-conscious in the presence of men, she *is* feeling angry and hateful. Her ways of defending against and avoiding such feelings are not working very well and she is in a corner. Perhaps the only way out, though she will not know that she is doing this, is to turn all those feelings that she is barely aware of, and does not want, upon herself. If she could 'depress' herself and take herself out of this life — of the order and even perhaps from life itself — is this the way that the conflict could cease? Without knowing it, and certainly without having made a conscious decision to this effect, this seems to be exactly what is happening.

We are not told the sequel to Anne's story, though we can hope that her eruption and her Superior's concern for her will halt a sequence that could have a tragic ending. Leaving the order would be one way out, but suicide could be on the cards since it might seem preferable to struggling with the unknown world inside and outside her. This may happen, despite what it says to the world about despair and negation of life. Anne is 'supposed' to be believing in and proclaiming 'life abundant'[3] but is she actually capable of doing this?

Peter and Jane

Peter and Jane have several problems, which are clearly

getting worse. They are having difficulty sorting out their personal and professional boundaries, and it is worse for these two than it might be for some others since there are two of them at work and their days and times off are not coinciding. They seem also to be experiencing conflict between the 'duty' of a minister and his family to accept moves as they come, and their desire for a bit more security in their work situation or at least the possibility of *a* place of their own to which they can escape.

It also appears that there is a lot else going on in their situation, some of it perhaps not so obvious, that is not really being looked at and faced. Why has Peter's son suddenly resorted to shoplifting? Is he picking up some of his parents' insecurity, or is something more complicated and obscure going on?

Could the mechanism of *projective identification*[4] be operating here, with Jonathan somehow acting as the rubbish dump for the bad and shameful things in the whole family? His father feels he has to be the perfect minister who couldn't possibly be having problems with his wife, nor bear to think of having to go through the pains and problems of a divorce. Peter is trying to stay all-good and since this is an impossibility the bad is somehow coming out in his son. We recall, too, that Peter has an episode in his own past of doing something bad and being humiliated for it. It is quite possible that he is *repressing* or *denying* this memory and consciously feeling even more cross with his son for somehow stirring this part of his depths. Unfortunately for Peter's feelings several people know about the shoplifting. He knows they have *said* that they feel sympathetic, but do they really? Do they not really secretly despise him and his son? We know that Peter is vulnerable to being humiliated; maybe what is happening is that he is feeling this again, despising himself and assuming that this is also what other people are doing. Again confusion is created in that this feeling of his may or may not be a *projection*; he is certainly likely to project his feelings of despising himself on to others, but they could actually be thinking it too. For it is often more comfortable to see 'bad' in somebody else than have to face the real possibility of 'there but for the grace of God go I'. In this particular case there may also be a lot of anger mixed up in it all for Peter is jeopardizing the *stereotype* and myth of the 'perfect' minister and the congregation may be furious about this.

The same difficulty arises over the possibility of the marriage breaking up. What would the congregation actually think? Peter *feels* it would be the end of his career, and the stark reality is that there is some danger that it might be. Peter has a *stereotype* that ministers' marriages can't and mustn't break down, and it is more than possible that his congregation shares this. In this very confused picture of feelings that may be going on both within Peter and between Peter and his congregation it is likely that what is being defended against is a great deal of *anxiety,* on all sides. And while this has to be kept down it will be very difficult for anybody to sort out who thinks or would think what.

Then we have to turn to Jane's part in the picture. We do not know how justified she is in her complaints that Peter is married to anyone and anything but her. It is unlikely that it has no basis in reality for the occupational hazard of ministry is that ministers are so often better at ministering to others than to themselves and their nearest and dearest. She says spitefully that Peter could even be having an affair, because he is caught up in a particular parishioner's bereavement situation. Is it actually that she is feeling deeply uncertain about herself and of being wanted by Peter when all seems to be going wrong, and, being unable to voice this, has gone over to the attack? Her own father was a doctor who was always being called out and often not there to say 'good-night' to her as a child because other people were sick and needed him more. It may be that she is too quick to see in Peter memories of her father which trigger off feelings of hurt and jealousy that she had or *denied* having as a child, and that she cannot consciously recognize the parallel. Or does she rightly sense that Peter can sometimes get over-involved, even if not in the way she fears? Perhaps Peter is having difficulty over the boundaries of pastoral duty and care and how to draw the line when a person is in such need. We do not know, but the question is there.

To make matters worse Peter is also having feelings about Jane going back to work, and so not being entirely available to share his overriding concern and interest for his work as his mother had always done. There are two possibilities here.

Firstly, that it really was as he remembered it, that mother did all the housework and nurtured the rest of the family without thought of her own needs, in which case it may well have been very difficult for him when Jane started being very different from the woman of his past experience. Or, secondly, perhaps it wasn't quite like that: perhaps mother did work and wasn't always available, and this was difficult and painful for him as a child. So difficult that he has needed to *deny* this part of his experience and remember it as having been some other way.

Once more we do not have enough information to know, but I hope we have raised enough possibilities to illustrate the point of how complex and confusing such a situation can become. There is probably a lot more anger and bitter disillusionment in this couple than either of them are aware of. Some of this is likely to belong not to the present situation, but to represent unresolved experiences, feelings and conflicts from the past to do with their relationships towards the formative men and women in their lives, namely their respective parents. The defences of *repression* and *denial* have been called into operation. The clue to them, if they can recognize it, could be their sullen, defiant son. One thing is certain; they need some clarity and insight if Jane's threat is not to become reality.

Elizabeth

The first thing to note about Elizabeth is that she lives all the time with a conflict between duty and desire, and between personal integrity and what people expect of her just by virtue of her being a woman minister who would like to be ordained to the priesthood, but is attached to a church which does not allow this. In fact she has been handling this conflict reasonably well, getting on with the job and accepting philosophically what for her are setbacks in the debate. But it is unwise to underestimate the low-lying and low-level stress that such a situation induces. There are signs, moreover, such as her increasing participation in movements favouring the ordination of women, that her desire is getting stronger. It may well have been only a matter of time before it got out of balance with her sense of duty and obedience to the Church and started causing more acute distress to her.

We cannot tell if this would have been so, for life itself overtook her when several things all happened at once. There was the death of her father and the associated necessity for increased relationship with a brother with whom she had never got on. Then there were the changes within her team ministry. One colleague left for a preferment she cannot look forward to, and another one started and within a year was to attain the very thing she has been trying to accept can never be hers. It is possible that one or other of these events alone — either the personal or the professional — would have been manageable; after all she has a history of dealing with conflict fairly equably. It is the *combination* of personal and professional which seems to have proved too much.

This is a different form of the personal/professional dimension to those encountered previously. It was not brought about by Elizabeth herself getting muddled or blurring the boundaries. Two life events juxtaposed themselves. It may therefore be more difficult to recognize and understand the possible interaction between them and Elizabeth's subsequent state, and she herself is probably quite unaware of it. But looking in from outside, as it were, we cannot but see that in both the personal and professional contexts the same configurations are repeated.[5] In both there is a younger brother or his equivalent; in a heightened state of awareness to her family it is likely that Elizabeth will *project* on to her colleague some aspects of the relationship with her brother, and probably the unpleasant ones since she is being forced to relate more to her brother in reality. In both there is a father who cannot comfort in a time of distress. Her actual father cannot because he is dead, and to some extent the cause of her distress. Indeed we know that Elizabeth has been bereaved, but this does not feature prominently in her story, and we can question as to whether this is because she has relegated or even *repressed* her grief and it is coming out in another way. The other 'father', her vicar, is simply not in touch with her distress and does not understand. In fact he is surprised at the intensity of Elizabeth's feelings because they are out of character, as well he may be if they do not all belong to the actual relationship with him, but relate back to her relationship with her father. A process of *projecting* on to and into could be going on. If he could have recognized this things could have gone differently, but that is perhaps a bit too much to ask, for he is the leader of a big working team and not, in his own eyes, a father-figure anyway. His pastoral interests have inclined him towards management rather than counselling, and in any case Elizabeth is his colleague not his client. How much further *could* he have gone without getting into a muddle over boundaries, and being too intrusive into Elizabeth's personal life, which after all is not really his concern . . . or is it? Are not vicars, bishops, etc., supposed to care and be fathers-in-God not only to lay people, but to their own kind? A thorny question rears its head here: who *does* care for the carers?

To Elizabeth, however, a very nasty feeling is making itself felt — jealousy, or even its more sinister brother, envy. This feeling is not being helped by the support of *her* own people; in a way that simply fuels the fire. She has never thought she has this in her, she who has always prided herself on being — well, not *always* nice — but not extreme, and certainly not vulnerable to one of the 'mortal' sins. To us, looking on, it appears that this 'not getting on with her brother' has always given a hint of darker, stronger feelings that she has dealt with by some sort of 'forgetting', perhaps a mixture of *denial* and *projection,* for she has always thought that if anything he was jealous of her.

The problem for Elizabeth, like Anne, is that her defences are crumbling and she is having to experience the feelings. What is she to do with them, since there seems to be no help available from anyone in the immediate situation? She thinks of the avoiding action of moving jobs, but this is a very dead end and she does just manage to see this, and redoubles her efforts to deal with things 'spiritually'. This, however, puts a strain on her inner being, even without her knowing it, so the other escape route comes in rather dramatically when she experiences a panic attack. For if there are too many awful, unacceptable and frightening feelings *inside* her and there is no obvious way of quietening them down, one solution is, as it were, to get rid of them *outside* herself, that is to *project* them on to the world about her. Perhaps it is marginally easier to be frightened of the supermarket than to be frightened of herself, though what on earth is going to happen in the long term? Supermarkets and the outside world are not going to go away, and shopping must be done if eating and living are to continue.

Jealousy and anger seem to have a terrific power over Elizabeth — their very presence can make her feel, indirectly, that she is going mad. They are of course 'very unchristian' and so is not being able to put up with a bit of frustration. 'Vocation and ministry are about service, not your own personal and professional fulfilment' — thus speaks the voice of conscience, which for Elizabeth has taken on almost the role of an internal judge or even persecutor. We might well ask questions about her relationship with her dead father since she seems to see God as so strict and harsh. Would she be as tough on any of her parishioners if they came to her with a similar story? She has always preached sermons on the love of God, but there have often been hints of conditions: He demands good behaviour back, or else . . . Her own state is going to make sermons on love more difficult to preach just now, since her experience currently is that if you are all nasty and bad inside no one is going to understand and love you. Yet she *has* always been able to proclaim comfort to others, and now they expect it of her. Can she go on doing it whilst feeling such conflict in herself without resorting to a potentially very unhealthy *splitting* of what she says from her personal being?

Robert

Robert has no problem as he sees it; it is only his annoying bishop and archdeacon who persist in giving him hints that he might have, or that he is not taking full advantage of the opportunities for fulfilment and growth that they have to offer. His brother also rather irritatingly keeps reminding him of an experience, not really a failure or anything, but just something a bit difficult in his past that he would really rather not think about. After all he is not ambitious; he leaves that to his brother. He didn't become a priest to get on in the world, or make a fuss when things don't go quite right for him.

The memory of his father laughing at him when he tried to

tell him about difficult teenage experiences sometimes obtrudes for a fleeting moment, and then luckily it goes away quickly. Besides, Yvonne, his wife, doesn't like him to be restless about the place; it disturbs her happy, settled, busy round as the vicar's wife, and he'd rather not be at the rough end of her impatience. Her behaviour seems to have an inordinately bad effect on him, but he doesn't stop to think that this is what he was used to from his mother throughout his childhood.

And he'd be better off not following through his theological ideas on the uniqueness of Christ; they didn't exactly serve him well in Birmingham. But anyway he wants to forget about all that . . .

Robert clearly has a lot of problems, the main one being that he is *denying* a lot of his past experience, and pushing it away if it does erupt into consciousness. The problem with this strategy is that he is experiencing a gradual deadening of himself inside; his hobbies are giving him no pleasure and he does not have any will to get on.

Maybe he has always had a sneaking idea that to be ambitious or innovative is wrong, perhaps because his brother does it so superlatively well and he could never have matched that. Being a vicar stopped that sort of direct competition, thank goodness, except that it didn't quite. He did feel innovative in Birmingham, and look what happened — a sort of failure — perhaps a punishment for the sin of watching to be successful and well-thought-of . . . better kept as a guilty secret, better still kept as a secret from himself because then he doesn't get those twinges of guilt. Maybe in fact he did want too much out of life? We may add the question of what happened to his natural desire for some recognition and encouragement from his parents as he began to enter the grown-up world. But that, like everything else, he has mostly forgotten, and particularly how it hurt sometimes.

In this situation the bishop doesn't have a chance. He is offering Robert precisely this sort of support and interest — he presumably knows about the Birmingham episode — but it is going to be rather difficult for Robert firstly to recognize it for what it is, secondly to believe in it and thirdly to accept it. His earlier experience gives the lie to such possibilities; they don't happen. This father-in-God is getting invested with feelings and attributes that really belong to another father, and the situation is reinforced because Yvonne tends to react in a way that is similar to his mother.[6]

There is quite a tangle here. The forbidden feelings may well be the *wanting* of care, affection and support and of being permitted to be innovative and ambitious, to compete with and even to beat his older brother. There had been a time in Birmingham when these drives broke through a bit, but with ultimately unpleasant consequences. So we have an instance of defences reasserting themselves; those of keeping self to self, not having too much interest in anything, not daring to hope for very much and indeed pretending not to want anything much.

To himself, Robert doesn't have problems. He does not have signs and symptoms of stress either, but he is in danger of drifting into a rut and of always living below the potential of his true self.

It is my hope that these extended vignettes have illustrated some of what the preceding chapter tried to set forth in a more theoretical way. They have shown up conflict both above and below the surface and I would now like to restate my conviction that attempts to understand and alleviate strain in ministry and upon ministers will be incomplete and unlikely to succeed without consideration of the hidden, unconscious dimension. This is because to the extent that it remains unconscious it is likely to operate as an ongoing source of confusion, distortion and frustration.

Of course not all hidden strain is *fully* unconscious and unknown to someone in the situation, though that which is causes the most difficulty. But there are also situations when the conflicts actually *are* conscious, but it suits some or all of the people involved 'not to know about them' and keep them very hidden.

The breakdown of clergy marriages and scandals involving individual clergy are such instances. It is commonplace for all concerned to get caught up in a conscious effort to preserve the good name of the minister, the Church or Synagogue, Religion itself or all three. Unfortunately this exercise usually involves a *denial* of what is really happening. Peter and Jane were becoming caught in this trap when their own personal investment in the situation became confused with that of their congregation. For stress and strain are felt more acutely when they cannot be acknowledged and shared; the cost to people of *denial* in order to preserve a 'good' image is considerable.

From these five stories several sorts of conflicts have emerged, often the same basic ones under different guises. These basic conflicts seem to me to cluster in three main areas.

First, there's a lot about *caring*; caring for others and caring or not caring for self. Second, we can identify a potential conflict engendered by the requirement to *proclaim,* consistently and publicly, a commitment to *relationship with God* and to a *belief — whatever* one's inner state. And third, the stories are shot through time and time again with the sense of a minister having to *be* a special sort of person, not only in the actual caring and proclaiming work, but in all areas of his or her professional and personal life.

The next chapters will therefore take up these three themes of *caring, believing* and *being* in an attempt to go beyond these five individuals into a more general reflection. The task is to start a dialogue between what actually goes on in our everyday life as ministers and the form and content of the religious tradition. The aim of such a dialogue is increased understanding and insight and decreased stress and strain.

Notes

1. See, for example, E. A. Locke 'Nature and causes of job satisfaction' in M. D. Dunnette, ed. *Handbook of Industrial and Organisational Psychology,* Chicago, Rand McNally Publishing Co. 1984, 2nd ed., and C. J. Cooper and R. Payne eds. *Stress at Work,* New York, Wiley 1978.
2. See also ch. 8, pp. 165—6.
3. As in John 10.10.
4. See ch. 3, pp. 63—4.
5. See ch. 9, pp. 169—71, 182.
6. See note 5.

FIVE

The Strain of Caring

In this chapter I want to look first at what goes into our human experience of caring, and then allow this to enter into dialogue with the religious tradition.

Our human experience of care and caring is one of the most fundamental of every human being, for the simple reason that we come into the world very small and helpless and quite incapable of caring for and fulfilling our own needs. We are dependent on mother, or on anyone who of necessity takes her place, for food, security, cuddling and almost all else. If parents cannot or will not provide this care then the child will be deprived, even sometimes to the point of death, but certainly to its general distress. An infant who is well cared for might be forgiven for thinking that its wish is everyone else's command. It has only to yell and things, usually gratifying and comforting, happen.

However, this idyllic existence cannot go on for ever for any child; it has to grow up and become a separate person. If there has been some breakdown in caring then this process may start out of due time. Be that as it may, every human being also learns what it is like to be apparently without care, or to have it taken away. Mother is not always on tap, and sometimes she even goes away when we actually want her, even though she comes back later. The likely natural reaction to this frustration, as can be observed in the behaviour of many infants, is an anger and rage which looks very uncomfortable for the one experiencing it. The puffed red face, clenched fists, holding of the breath and copious tears of a child in a state of frustration or deprivation are perfectly observable to all of us, and correspond to an inner experience we might wish to avoid having again in the future, and forget having had in the past.

The strength of the determination to avoid or to forget

depends, to an extent, on the consequences of our anger: whether we were understood, contained and held through it, or whether we were only scolded, told to 'shut up' or punished with withdrawal or even violence. The first experience can help us to integrate our anger constructively into our being; the second is likely to induce in us a feeling of the badness of that part of ourselves. If parents or others compound the situation by instilling into us how much they have been hurt by us, and even that God will not love us, then the desire to make amends, natural and normal in any child, becomes excessive. Somehow we have to show we care, and have to try to repair the damage we think we have done.

Herein lies the problem; our primitive, infantile feelings are intense, but the hostile reactions and actions to which they may give rise cannot, by reason of our smallness, normally be such as to cause extensive external damage. But since we lack the fully developed mental equipment to discuss and assess the situation, as adults can if they will, it becomes magnified out of all proportion to its actual reality. Our rage will be real *for us,* for it is our experience. The 'damage' we do, and thus our need to feel guilt will be much more fantasy than reality, but it is hard for us, at this stage of our development, even to begin to grasp that fantasy and reality are different.

Something of this process must happen to all of us, and most of us find some of these experiences too painful to remember in our adult life, so we defend ourselves against them by, most probably, *repression* or *denial* — by keeping them unconscious and so out of our awareness. To our defences against these painful feelings we may also need to add *reaction formation,* that is to practise, consciously, their very opposite. So we will be always giving rather than depriving others or wanting for ourselves, always being nice rather than nasty, upset or angry, and always placating so as not to be confronted by guilt. This may succeed very well, and we come to imagine that we are this sort of person.

If then we enter one of the 'caring' professions, and it may be attractive because it offers us great possibilities for reinforcing our 'nice' idea of ourselves, then the way of *projection* as a way of fending off our more painful feelings becomes very easily available to us. All deprivation, anger and helplessness can be seen as belonging to our clients, not to us; we can exercise caring and giving to the full without realizing that we are perhaps misidentifying our own sense of being in need of care with theirs. This has disadvantages both for our clients and ourselves. We may not be able to let our clients be free to grow because we are always caring for them and perhaps smothering them. For ourselves we find it difficult to desist, to take time off, to admit that sometimes we cannot succeed. For it is difficult to say 'no' to a client or parishioner, if in some way and on some level he or she is representing a part of ourselves — the needy part — for we know what being deprived feels like even if we have 'forgotten' we know.

Furthermore if, as is likely, it is not only deprived and helpless feelings but also angry feelings that we are afraid of and want to keep unconscious and so apparently 'far' from us, we are also likely to misidentify caring for people with pleasing them and avoiding any confrontation because it might bring anger into the situation. All this makes us tired and stressed, because it may not be taking note of reasonable external limits, and though we are unaware of it it is also straining our internal defences. However, we still manage reasonably well, provided that the other person is grateful or seems to be getting something from our care. The equilibrium of the system is preserved, and for a long while stress may stay manageable and even unnoticeable.

Suppose, however, that the recipients are not always grateful or are angry with us for not doing enough. That can reproduce for us a feeling of our earlier years when *we* inevitably did not get all we wanted. Our reaction, like that of our clients, was anger; when we see this painful, forgotten and 'forbidden' emotion in others what can we do to 'get things nice' again? We can redouble our efforts, but since most of us do not have the physical resources to do this for ever, sometimes and suddenly we do an about-turn. Our defence against 'non-niceness' and anger fails — sometimes rather thoroughly. Instead of identifying *with* our clients we find them intolerable; we *project* on to and into them selfish demand. We attack their ungratefulness and wish to be rid of the burden of caring for them. But all unwittingly we, in our turn, have had to experience for ourselves the dreaded emotion, anger. Because of this we can become guilty and redouble our efforts yet again. It does not take much imagination to see how the vicious circle of stress and exhaustion builds up. The two likely catastrophic end-points are either an inappropriate and uncontrollable anger, episodic or smoulderingly resentful, or an emotional or physical giving up.

Naturally not all caring professionals will get into this state; whether they do so or not will depend on the severity of earlier experience, the strength of the defences used and the events that happen in life. But something of this experience is inevitable for all of us. It is not necessarily true to say that those entering the helping professions do so primarily to fulfil their own unconscious needs; that would be to go beyond the evidence. But it probably *is* fair to suggest that those in the helping professions may well experience reverberations from unresolved parts of themselves to do with caring, and will need, for their own physical and emotional health, to come to terms with them — probably not immediately, but perhaps with the first failure in a hitherto successful career, or a prolonged exposure to something like the inner-city situation where the problems are unavoidably larger than an individual's resources.

We see that unconscious and *projected* deprivation, not wanting to care, anger, helplessness and guilt can cause difficulty for those in the caring professions. The likely form that this will take will be to defend against the painful feelings by *denial, projection* and/or *reaction formation* until and unless those defences break under pressure. Religious ministry is, historically and in fact, the caring profession *par excellence:* its stated task is 'the cure (care) of souls (people)'. So ministers are likely to demonstrate something of denial, projection and/or reaction formation. If we return to our five people, can we come to identify some of these factors in a conscious or nearly conscious form, or have we any thoughts as to what may be going on unconsciously?

The first thing we notice is that they all seem to have some difficulty in caring for themselves, and particularly in understanding *compassionately* what is happening to them. Furthermore, this lack of understanding goes over into *action* in the way that they behave towards themselves and that others behave towards them. Anne continues to drive herself rather than admit to anyone that life is pretty tough. Peter and Jane, though worried, find it difficult to care for their nearest and dearest in the shape of their son when he goes off the rails. They experience him as sullen and defiant, and seem unable to reach him emotionally. Elizabeth does, it is true, try to ask for some understanding for herself, but for her it is more that her vicar seems not to be able to take seriously the fact that she needs it. We have admitted that there may well be difficulties for him in providing this care himself, but we notice that he does not point her in any other direction, but implicitly expects her to get over it as usual. Robert's bishop and archdeacon do have some real concern for him, but he is very unwilling to receive it; his family background, in particular, makes it very difficult for him to acknowledge his need. It may be, too, that this bishop, though well-intentioned, is not skilled enough in finding ways to communicate his concern sensitively and effectively. It is not always most helpful to express this by suggesting that a man needs further training — this could come over as a threat and set up the feeling of 'They think I'm not good enough'. Robert's brother, too, offers concern in a way that could be seen as tinged with more than a little triumph at his own more successful position, and as containing an implicit sense of contempt: 'You haven't got very far, have you?'

Given the sense in which caring professionals may have *split off* their own neediness, *projected* it on to others and reinforced this by seeing themselves as the givers and carers *par excellence,* thus setting up a very strong overall defence against vulnerability, more, rather than less, sensitivity needs to go into the process of providing care for the carers.

It is still more difficult for caring professionals to get in touch with and tolerate their frustration and anger with the business of caring and, ultimately, with *not wanting to care.* It may take exhaustion or illness to make them stop, and these particular ways of stopping allow us to say, 'I had to stop caring, I was too tired and I got ill', rather than to look at the possibility 'I became ill, exhausted, etc., because I was sick and fed up with giving all the time and not getting much back, and was not able to admit this even to myself.'

We have already noticed this conflict in John. He did have

moments, confusing to him, of wanting to dodge his parishioners and finding their demands intolerable, but it looks as if he was unable to handle these feelings in himself. He felt, we suppose, guilty about having them and sometimes had then to redouble his efforts at caring. The churning turbulence and confusion of feeling inside him finally went to his tummy and showed itself as disturbance there. Anne has not even got quite as far as John, perhaps because from childhood on she was always used to being the care-giver. We get no hint from her story that she is plagued by feelings of not caring for her school-children or sisters in her community; in fact all her overt striving is towards making more effort to care. But she does find herself caught in angry feelings and the very depressive sense that life is not worth living.

It is interesting, though, that she, John and Elizabeth begin to manifest feelings of uncertainty and turbulence in another, more external direction. John has doubts about his faith and his training, Anne wonders about the reforms of Vatican II and whether the religious life is really right for her, and Elizabeth toys with the idea of changing the external situation by looking for another job. She does, though, also realize that given the current restrictions on women's ministry the same old feelings of frustration and jealousy are likely to recur. But there is a tendency in all of them to another form of *projection,* namely to define the problem in terms of the external situation and of factors outside themselves.

This is a tricky area for there are *real* issues and questions here. There *are* gaps and inadequacies in theological training, there *are* questions to be asked about the structures of the religious life, and there *are* inherent limitations to women's ministry in the Church of England. I am not wanting to suggest that every external move in and out of religious life or forms of ministry could be avoided if people sorted out their internal emotional problems; that would be simplistic and to deny real external factors. In fact, working through some of these factors can in itself mean imperative and inevitable changes in forms of life and ministry. This is most likely to happen if the original response to a sense of vocation was made in a state of unawareness of a person's self, of his or her needs and of parts of his or her personality. But if such changes are made in desperation and as a last-ditch measure without achieving more awareness, the whole pattern is likely to be repeated. Such would be the danger of John, Anne or Elizabeth making precipitate external changes in their respective situations. For true care for self needs to go beyond the external and look towards an inner understanding and compassion.

Yet it is precisely this empathy and compassion that ministers often exercise very well in respect to others and very badly in respect to themselves. They sometimes have great difficulty in taking themselves and their feelings seriously; we suspect that Peter and Jane are much more worried deep down by their constant job changes and lack of a permanent home than they can admit to themselves. It is well recognized that moving job and home is a major stressful life event[1] but it is so often seen as just a normal part of ministry. Acknowledging feelings of insecurity and resentment of the system will not, of itself, change anything external, but it can reduce some of the inner strain. In this case it may even be that Peter's son is reacting, more than the rest of the family, to the prospect of yet another move. We do not know, but the question is worth asking.

The other area in which ministers of religion are notoriously bad at caring for themselves is in their response to a 'received' dictum of total availability and a merging of personal and professional such as would not be tolerated by many other people. John shows this in his initial inclination not to be fussy about his days off, and to have his vicarage door always open. Jane's complaint that Peter is married to everything but her probably has some truth in it, and Robert is not heeding the warning signs that his enthusiasm for his favourite off-duty pastimes is going dead, like the rest of him.

There is a question as to why these people, and many others, are blurring the boundaries so much? Caring professionals are often lonely; the need for confidentiality about their work and, sometimes, just this unacknowledged sense of being uncared for in themselves — as well as more obvious causes such as actually living alone — all contribute. Blurring the boundaries between work and personal life may by a way of staving off loneliness in terms of time and can mask a sense of personal worthlessness and emptiness. 'If I stay in the role, people will want me; they might not just for myself', goes the inner, often unacknowledged dialogue. So we never really face ourselves or our deep-seated fears and doubts. Furthermore, to make 'half'-friends of the people we serve and care for — realizing that this places some limitation on friendship — can equally hide more fundamental fears about human intimacy and closeness. Because we are always 'half' in our professional role it is always there for us to retreat into; we can fend people off if they threaten to come too close and so protect our own vulnerability — though this manoeuvre is often very hurtful to the person at the other end of the process. Blurring boundaries, therefore, may be embraced as both a solution to and a defence against our inner conflicts, but it creates, in the long term, far more problems than it solves.

We turn now to *anger* as a potentially major stumbling block in the process of caring. We can see this in Anne: it is quite possibly her inability to come to terms with her angry feelings that is making her exhausted and depressed. John oscillates between allowing his angry feelings full sway and then guiltily redoubling his efforts at caring and not being angry. Jane is more angry than Peter: it is she who is threatening rejection, while Peter is more surprised and hurt, partly guilty perhaps, but covering this with self-justification and an assertion of how much compromise and adjustment he has already made. Elizabeth is more aware of jealousy than anger, but there is a hint in her of the more sinister envy, the near-hate for her younger colleague and perhaps a forbidden wish to destroy him; we see this when we are told that she is not helped by people expressing sympathy for her, that this only fuels her fire. We have to ask: the fire of what?

Robert is so cut off from all his feelings, other than a mild irritation that people will not let him alone, that it is difficult to know what he really feels. But we note that he is at some pains not to incense what he calls the 'impatience' of Yvonne his wife. Strong negative feelings in someone else are clearly not something he wants to invite; it may be also that if he himself let himself feel them then they would be very uncomfortable and even overwhelming.

To a degree all except Robert, who is again well protected by his defences, feel *helpless,* Anne and Elizabeth perhaps the most so since both feel in a trap, and neither knows what to do about it. Elizabeth failed in her effort to get help; Anne was unable to take any initiative and required that other people should notice her distress. John and Peter do not, at first sight, seem quite so helpless. John has decided that he is physically ill and needs treatment; at least there is an avenue open there. Jane and Peter are at the quarelling stage where threats and recommendations for action are being made. But underneath, these two are experiencing the helplessness of not understanding what is happening to them; this would become more manifest if their present strategies fail.

What is striking is that they have all gone to some lengths to avoid this helpless feeling: John's vicious and oscillating circle of activity, Anne's valiant efforts to continue as usual, Elizabeth's philosophical attitude to an unremittingly frustrating situation and Robert's studied invulnerable attitude are all such manoeuvres.

Some of them feel *guilty* — notably Anne, Elizabeth and to an extent Peter — but the extent and level of their guilt is not very clear. Is it because they are failing their own expectations of themselves, their superiors, their parishioners or God?

It looks as if the feelings and experiences of our five people tally with those of other caring professionals who get into difficulties, though we have also isolated some additional features in the work of ministry which may add to the strain. We need to ask now whether there are factors in the *religious tradition* that are likely to mitigate or exacerbate the situation. It could emerge that in some ways the tradition and inheritance of religion 'protects' the minister, in the sense of allowing certain feelings into consciousness and making them easier to bear. But we may also find that in other ways the pressure of the tradition is instrumental in driving certain experiences and feelings deeper underground, making them more inaccessible to the person's awareness and so more likely to sap energy and reverberate in unpleasant ways.

I would like, therefore, to turn now to the religious and biblical tradition, in order to start a dialogue. We have already seen, in Chapter 2, that there is a *general climate* in the religious tradition of the Church as boundless care-giver. We noted instances of uncaring but did not probe them beyond citing the extreme reaction of anger they occasion in those outside the Church. I hope that this present chapter may have clarified a little what humanly goes into these strong feelings about caring and uncaring. The reflection in Chapter 2 was focused on ministers in general as they function as representatives of total religious bodies. I now want to look more at specific figures from the tradition to see if, as individuals, they show something of the same sorts of feelings and conflicts as have emerged in this present chapter. I am thinking of St Paul, the prophet Elijah and Martha of the Martha and Mary stories.

The following passages may be allowed to speak for themselves: . . . 'when I was with you and was in want, I did not burden any one . . . So I refrained and will refrain from burdening you in any way';[2] 'I will not be a burden . . . I will most gladly spend and be spent for your souls'[3]; 'We are treated as imposters, and yet are true.'[4] Here we see in St Paul, intent on caring, the pushing away of his own neediness and resentment at the reaction he gets — all covered with attempts at self-justification.

If we turn to the prophet Elijah we see variations on the same theme, but his anger and bitterness are primarily directed against God: 'I have been very jealous for the Lord, the God of hosts; for . . .[they have] slain thy prophets with the sword; and I, even I only am left; and they seek my life, to take it away.'[5] After all he has done for God, what has he got from it? Simply that his life is forfeit.

If we go to the story of Mary and Martha we find a similar state of affairs: 'But Martha was distracted with much serving; and she went to him and said, "Lord, do you not care that my sister has left me to serve alone? Tell her then to help me." '[6]

Martha feels that she has been left to do all the work of caring and her resentment and bitterness are palpable, together with her jealousy and envy of Mary. Jesus then reminds her, perhaps not in so many words but it is implied, to take care of herself.

So we see that these most devoted servants and carers seem to have been subject to rather similar emotions to those we have already isolated. The human predicament of getting caught in too much caring is not unknown in the Bible. But there is another strand in the biblical tradition which perhaps lies at the root of why it is so difficult for servants and apostles of God not to try to care without limits. For alongside the purely human there lives the 'threat' of the 'more than human'. We see it in the prophet Isaiah: 'Behold my servant, whom I uphold . . . I have put my spirit upon him . . . He will not cry or lift up his voice . . . a bruised reed he will not break . . . He will not fail or be discouraged . . .'[7]

The example of the servant, as exemplifying the care and activity of God, is a daunting one for any human minister. Then, as we already noted in Chapter 2, there is the 'threat' of the teaching and example of Christ: 'If any one forces you to go one mile, go with him two miles. Give to him who begs from you . . .'[8]

The prescription is to care and give without stinting and without concern for oneself. This is reiterated in the 'demands' of the 'last discourses' of St John's Gospel which are almost frightening in their standard and intensity: 'This is my commandment, that you love one another as I have loved you. Greater love has no man than this, that a man lay down his life for his friends.'[9]

The injunction, here, to unlimited sacrificial care and love is total and daunting to 'ordinary' human ministers and carers. So it is difficult in this climate to acknowledge the need for care in ourselves or, worse still, to admit our own uncaringness. Then we have, throughout the New Testament, the injunction to put away all anger and bitterness.[10] Anger is often referred to as one of the cardinal sins and in the Songs of the Suffering Servant[11] and the stories of the passion of Christ we see, if we read them one way, no anger but only submission. Anger is to be avoided; it belongs only to other people, like those who crucified the Lord. Even in the Old Testament where the anger of *men* seems more 'allowed' there is still the spectre of the terrible 'wrath of God'.

It is difficult, therefore, to resist carrying away from the Bible a reinforcement of our sense that anger is destructive. Against this background we easily 'forget' the anger of Jesus in the cleansing of the Temple,[12] or the anger of Moses with Israel.[13] We miss the sense of Isaiah and other prophets who see anger as giving the strength for further effort and achievement and for getting things done in the face of opposition or oppression. Anger remains outlawed for us, and so, often, *split off* from the rest of our being.

Guilt features prominently in the Bible. It should be said that most of the Old Testament sacrifices are not propitiatory as people have been wont to think, but should be interpreted as the means of *offering* life. But there is a certain amount of material, from Genesis onwards, which seems to encourage man to feel guilty before God. Adam and Eve feel guilty when faced by God's question of 'Adam, where are you?'. They hide their faces. Many of the psalms, for example Psalm 51,[14] talk of man's guilt before God, and in the New Testament we have, among others, the story of the sin, guilt and subsequent forgiveness of Peter.[15] Guilt, unlike anger, is almost hallowed in the Bible; it is the way to forgiveness by God. This, in turn, may make it a more bearable emotion for our human consciousness. We can allow it in ourselves, even to excess.

Helplessness, too, is not unknown in the Bible. Job is rendered helpless before the majesty of God,[16] though it comes out all right in the end! *Dependence* (on God at any rate) is everywhere, together with an apparent exaltation of submission and weakness: 'my power is made perfect in weakness',[17] or 'the weakness of God is stronger than men'.[18] So feelings about caring, not caring, anger, dependence, helplessness and guilt are all present in the Bible. I say 'feelings', rather than thoughts or ideas, deliberately. Exegesis of the relevant passages on an intellectual level may be able to remove some inconsistencies and produce some logical coherence of thought, but I am submitting that despite our rational thinking there is a general 'climate' within the biblical tradition which somehow conveys to us the sense that anger is dangerous and bad, while guilt and dependence on God (though not necessarily on human beings) are OK. If this is in any sense true it cannot help but have an effect, not always acknowledged or understood, on us who are the inheritors of that tradition.

If we generalize this and let it come into dialogue with our humanness and psychological awareness we get something like the following: the problem of anger for caring professionals is likely to be intensified for those in the Christian, if not the Jewish, tradition of ministry. We have seen that anger comes to be feared, experientially, by many people. This fear is there in a muted form in the Old Testament. It is muted because it is the more remote wrath of

God which is feared; anger between human beings is more acceptable. In the New Testament and subsequent writings there is more of a *split* on the human level. One strand of Christianity which seems to extol love, joy and peace sees anger only in other people — historically, for example, in those seen as responsible for the death of Christ. This allows both minister and people to label anger as bad and to *split* it off from themselves, and this *splitting* is made more absolute by an emphasis on God as pure love and goodness, without any darkness at all. The humanly dreaded thing becomes more awful, for it is outside the embrace of God as well as man. God can therefore 'become' the equivalent of the parent who cannot contain rage and destructiveness, which in its turn prevents us accepting them back and integrating them into our being.

On an everyday level all can go well unless things happen that make ministers want to feel angry, either with something personal, or with something that is going on between them and their congregations. They have then either to deny their anger altogether, thus risking depression or breakdown, or to see it as totally righteous, like that of Christ in the temple, so that other people are in the wrong. In the latter case, this unallowed anger can be expressed against so-called immoral people, or in taking a fairly violently aggressive stand for or against 'causes'; but it is then seen as not really anger, but righteous indignation. In other words, anger has to be *denied* or *renamed.* Ministers who claim that all their anger is righteous indignation may not subjectively experience strain and stress, but those who are beginning to take responsibility by calling anger by its name can come into sharp conflict with their parishioners or community. On the other hand, ministers who persist in denying anger and are always 'nice' are likely to arouse such frustration in their less defended associates, who object to having to feel all the anger themselves, that *they* may become violent and attacking. All this is extremely stressful and it is not hard to see where some aspect of it may have been operating in some of our five characters. But the point I am wanting to make now is that it can be a pretty widespread phenomenon in one form or another. If anger cannot be understood and worked with it will get out of hand;

the only other way is to 'outlaw' it completely, psychologically and theologically.

In contrast, guilt will not *apparently*[19] be so much of a problem, and so will cause less stress, just because the tradition seems to 'allow' it. It is therefore possible to admit and channel past and current occasions or fantasies of guilt into a sense of sin before God and one's neighbour; sin can then be forgiven and human helplessness contained within the activity of God. I would like to try to illustrate what I mean by a personal example.

During a European pastoral care and counselling conference in Lublin, Poland, in 1981 we were taken to visit the concentration camp of Majdanek. The group included both Jews and Christians and people from every European country, so the experience was potentially and in actuality both intense and very painful. We were shorn of any 'religious dimension' for the camp stands starkly as it was with no chapel, nothing. Many of us felt guilty — for differing and obscure reasons — and it became a unique opportunity for each of us to explore the darker reaches of ourselves and of human beings in general, though I do not know what each of us made of it and what opportunities we, individually, took or missed, for it was hard to talk about afterwards. But what I do remember was what seemed to be a corporate sense of relief when we could join in prayers of penitence in the crematorium. *In invoking God something of the weight of our human sense of guilt and helplessness was lightened.*

This illustration is extreme and indeed does give both sides of the coin: on the one hand, because we were the kind of group we were we could honestly draw upon the religious dimension at that moment. On the other, confronted by Majdanek we could not just tune into our religious heritage and 'drown' guilt in love without first encountering what underlay that guilt. But in more ordinary situations within the security of the everyday life and liturgy of the religious community I think we can, and sometimes do.

The very process of seeking forgiveness from God may obscure what is really happening inside ourselves. If the consciousness of guilt is much more sustained than that of the feelings that tend to give rise to it, such as anger, hate, greed and envy we can go on dealing 'religiously' — through confession and forgiveness — with our more unacceptable and disliked feelings, without really coping with the experience of them at a human level. The religious process, almost programme, can serve to *deny* their full emotional impact on consciousness and so leave them smouldering away in our unconscious. So stress and strain build up and never get confronted because the underlying feelings are being 'anaesthetized' rather than truly 'contained' by the religious tradition.

I am *not,* by this, meaning to imply a rejection of the process of forgiveness as experienced in the religious traditions. Rather I am asking that we should have a greater psychological awareness of what, humanly, goes into it. If we are to be released from the sometimes poisonous and destructive effects of some of our feelings and actions we need first to be enabled to know, emotionally, what they are. It is not that forgiveness is unhelpful — far from it — but an over-quick and over-programmed experience of forgiveness may be. It may actually impede our growth in compassion and a full ability to care.

Towards *dependence*[20] we tend to be ambivalent. Dependence on God is to be encouraged, perhaps because we fashion him in the likeness of a truly reliable parent. Dependence on fallible human beings is far more fraught — our childhood experience showed us that, and we cannot help but notice that ministers often show a great resistance to *receiving* help from others.

In summary, I am suggesting that ministers of religion, like many other caring professionals, tend to *project* out from themselves both their need for care *and* the unpleasant feelings associated with not getting it, or not enough of it. Moreover, the impact of the religious tradition means that this human 'cycle' works in a particular way which we need to explore and try to understand.

Yet 'caring', though a vital part of ministry, is not the whole of ministry. Inherent in our mandate is the witness to and proclamation of a dimension that in some sense transcends material and current reality. This has its own intrinsic possibilities of stress and strain and it is to these that we turn in the next chapter.

Notes

1. T. H. Holmes and R. H. Rahe Social Readjustment Rating Scale, *Journal of Psychosomatic Research*, 11 (1967), pp. 213−18.
2. 2 Corinthians 11.9.
3. 2 Corinthians 12.14−15.
4. 2 Corinthians 6.8.
5. 1 Kings 19.14.
6. Luke 10.40.
7. Isaiah 42.1−4.
8. Matthew 5.41−2.
9. John 15.12−13.
10. Ephesians 4.31.
11. Particularly Isaiah 52.13 to 53.12.
12. Mark 11.15ff.
13. Exodus 32.19; Numbers 16.15.
14. Psalm 51, especially vv. 1−4.
15. Luke 22.55−62 and John 21.15−19.
16. For instance Job 19.8 or Job 40.4.
17. 2 Corinthians 12.9.
18. 1 Corinthians 1.25.
19. See also ch. 8, pp. 154−6.
20. See also ch. 8, pp. 150−2.

SIX

The Strain of Relating to God

**The ultimate milieu of faith — Encounter
with omnipotence**

> Immensity cloystered in thy deare wombe,
> Now leaves his wellbelov'd imprisonment.[1]

These opening lines of John Donne's sonnet encapsulate
the heart of what I call the great *confusion* of our religious
faith and life. Donne's context is the nativity, but I want to
allow the lines to 'float free' of this. Whose immensity, whose
womb and whose cloistering? We attempt to relate to the
immensity of God, but from where do we get our sense of him
and the task?

I feel that it cannot but come from the deeply-buried
memory of our own infant past when we emerged into a
world to relate to another in a new, more distinct way, for we
had hitherto been inside her and a part of her. In that first
period of our totally dependent infant lives what confusion
could we have told of if only we had had the words to put to
it? Is the world outside us — her world/our world still, for we
cannot be separate from her — the source of our bliss or the
source of our helpless pain and rage? We cannot tell for it
seems to change according to whether she is there or not
there for us. When she is there her world merges with us in
the periodic renewal of excitement, satisfaction and
tranquillity; perhaps we could come to feel that the source of
all power and life is in *us*? When she is withdrawn from us all
seems helplessness and nothingness inside us, and 'outside'
is a great all-encompassing threateningness.

With the passage of time through infancy and childhood
this experience becomes inaccessible to us, yet it lives on
inside as an inexpressible memory. In adult life we can have,
as it were, opaque 'windows' on to this scene. The world of

madness is one such 'window', and another is, I suggest, the world of religious faith. Both are potentially worlds of great excitement and great fear, for in them we encounter great forces which we can locate both within and without us.

When we live in or around the world of religious faith we want to keep it from becoming, for us, the world of madness. We have to try to contain the uncontainable, and in the Old Testament the Song of Songs and the book of Job bear witness to this dimension. The former expresses it within the ecstasy of love[2] — ecstatic, but still somehow contained, but the latter shows us the God who, having deprived Job of everything, confronts him with an annihilating sense of omnipotence: 'Then the Lord answered Job out of the whirlwind . . . Who then is he who can stand before me?'[3]

Job can only repent before this majesty in dust and ashes.[4]

Such, I feel, is the *ultimate* context of our relationship with God, and it is within this context that I want to set what follows.

The 'imprisonment' of immensity — a necessary constraint?

Religious people have a concern with God which in some form or another has pervaded man's conscious and unconscious thought through the ages. The Jewish tradition and the Christian Church have given a particular 'shape' to this concern. Their collective experience has accumulated and lives on in a way that is in some sense independent of the individuals and groups who comprise the membership of Jewish and Christian bodies at any one time.

Consciously we call this 'living shape' the tradition. But I think it also represents, at one and the same time, our *unconscious* need to give a boundary and structure to our encounter with the Unknown, with Omnipotence — which is both inside and beyond us.

The New Testament itself is perhaps the strongest example of a boundary that is given to us from 'outside'. The proclamation of the incarnation of God in Christ, 'he who has seen me has seen the Father'[5] puts a defining boundary on God, and we note here Michael Ramsey's commentary in

God, Christ and the World when he says, 'God is Christ-like, and in Him is no non-Christlikeness at all'.[6] The proclamation of the New Testament and its injunction to live out the example of Christ are, it seems to me, trying to 'bring us up' from an encounter with the dark primitive force of naked omnipotence into a more developed, 'safer' realm where the personal is paramount and the primitive is contained within the experience of forgiveness and reparation and the practice of love and compassion.

Even here, however, the other side seeps through. 'In the beginning was the Word'[7] points us back to the creation stories of Genesis and the boundless strength and power of the Spirit of God. The rest of St John's Gospel removes the drama from the realms of the purely personal into that of the 'huge' uncontrollable themes of light and darkness, good and evil. And there has always survived in the later mystical tradition that which has *affirmed* the unknowable, unbounded nature of God, and our *inability* to comprehend it.

But we have indications in the Bible that an immediate sense of the unboundedness of God is too much for human beings. In the Old Testament there is the sense that we cannot see God and live[8]; he is usually mediated through the Shekinah — the glory of God, the cloud on Mount Sinai, or even more concretely by the pillar of fire and the pillar of smoke[9]. There are hints in Genesis 3[10] that the knowledge of good and evil, coming through the eating of the fruit of the Tree of Life, is particularly dangerous for human beings; the threat is death and it actually results in expulsion from paradise and a life of toil where previously there had been only bliss.

On the *human* level we can see the Fall stories as representing humankind getting in touch with more of itself, the parts we do not know about, our unconscious power, and in the stories this is located in sexuality. It seems that this exploration brings about the wrath of God and consequent expulsion from paradise.

There is, however, another possibility. God's question to Adam in the garden was not, as might have been expected, given the fact that Adam and Eve had done what they were not supposed to do, 'Adam, what have you done?', but the far more open question, 'Adam, where are you?'[11] Adam responds in shame and hides himself — he cannot face himself or Yahweh at that point — and it is at least possible that it is this sense of shame and not the act itself that brought about the separation process. Be that as it may, it has the effect that the dwelling-place of God is put outside the reach of man; is it not possible that we have internalized this mythological event in ourselves and seen it as putting a barrier and a prohibition on *all* our exploring, when perhaps separation and alienation come when we fear to *face and confront* our own exploring? We may have good reason for this fear because of the depth into which exploration could lead us, but cutting it off altogether cuts us off from a whole dimension of ourselves, and from our deepest roots.

It is interesting to note the commentaries of two of the Church Fathers on the Fall story. St Augustine, whose thought has more generally passed into the tradition, sees man as originally perfect, falling from this and becoming a 'mass of perdition'[12] essentially separate from God except through the redemptive activity of Christ. This is saying something very strong to our exploration in relation to God; we cannot reach Him and we are sinful if we overreach ourselves and try. St Irenaeus, incidentally writing two hundred years earlier,[13] sees man as 'born' primitive, both personally and collectively; we cannot but grow and develop and must explore in the process. To Irenaeus, the Fall is not a false and punishable first step, and our tendency to deviate from the ideal in this process of growth and exploration is inevitable, yet not inevitably disastrous. This summary is over-simplistic, as a detailed study of the Fathers would show, but I do not think it is so far off the mark as to be false and inapplicable.

Humanly speaking, these two attitudes could be seen as corresponding to the possible attitudes of both our parents towards us at a rather later stage of our development than that of the beginning of this chapter: the time when we have a self and want increasingly to explore and master the world outside us. There is and must be some fear that the child will overreach and damage himself. But whether this gets expressed as, 'Don't, you naughty child, you mustn't do that; I/God won't love you if you do', or whether it is expressed as, 'Go and have a try', and then, 'What happened, was it a bit hard for you?', can make all the difference as to whether we grow up fearful or secure towards ourselves and our need to explore and, ultimately, to our quest after meaning. Furthermore, the way we can negotiate this later stage will depend on how secure and contained we were during the earlier period of more total dependency.

Perhaps we can see something of the human basis of religious people's dilemma over faith and exploration. The divide and the tension between the need to explore and the need for secure boundaries to the essentially unfathomable have always been there. The ongoing tension is reflected in the controversy centering on the Bishop of Durham's statements in 1984 querying the traditional understanding of both the resurrection and the virgin birth.[14] Some people welcomed these; others reacted strongly against them, calling on the bishops for a restatement of the immutable heart of the Christian revelation and the nature of belief.

More indirectly we can see the tension in the controversy over the ordination of women, or in the life of the fundamentalist sects, though people may not be pleased that I am linking these together. I am doing so because of the *intensity* of the debate in both cases, resulting in a use of desperate warlike images. 'Battle looms on women priests' front' ran the headline in the *Church Times,*[15] and there is a considerable use of martial imagery in fundamentalist literature. The intensity of the need to know and hang on to the nature and activity of God suggests a fear, a fight for survival. It is a clue that we have 'descended' into the raw primitive area of our experience. People who challenge the 'known' truth need to be excluded and told they are out of line. Deep down, the fear seems to be of the chaos of the uncontrollable, and 'orthodox' belief a way to structure the chaos and make it both comprehensible and safer.

It may feel, even if I have not actually said so, that I am coming down on one side and saying that exploration is 'good' and somehow braver, and a desire for orthodoxy, certainty and a received tradition is 'bad'. Indeed I am by temperament an exploring sort of person, at least intellectually, and *consciously* find great difficulty in coping with limits that are set on exploration. But I do wonder if I can only be like this because I 'know' that there are people who are holding the other pole, the desire for and the affirmation of certainty, for me. It is as if I have done some *splitting* and *projecting*; perhaps I have put out from me on to other people my unconscious need, which I don't seem to like, for certainty and to be held by the tradition. I have to ask myself what I would do if the certain people and that strand in faith were not there. Similarly for the person inclined consciously the other way, towards a non-exploratory adherence to received truth: would this become limiting and frightening in its turn if people like me did not exist?

What I am trying to say is that just as all our personal past lies within us so the problem of faith and doubt is *within each of us*. In relation to God and religion we are exposing ourselves to the huge existential questions of meaning, chaos, being and nothingness. These questions cannot but be around for all of us, but the degree to which and the manner in which we address them varies, and in my opinion is deeply affected by our emotional make-up and experience. Some people do not address them at all, unless forced to by life events, death and unjust suffering being the most likely to arouse them. Others, such as Shakespeare, Sartre, Nietszche and other less well-known people cannot but address them all the time, often to their pain and discomfort. David Jenkins in *Guide to the Debate about God*[16] probably reflects the overall balance when he suggests that some people ask ultimate questions some of the time.

No doubt there is an interplay here with what is going on in the 'outside' world of the time. I think it is significant that there seems to be a resurgence of conservative religion and politics at a time when the frontiers of our existence are being pushed back in other ways, and the potential of this — both benign and malignant — becomes more fully seen. We have the conquest of space *and* the 'Star Wars' programme, the discovery of the energy of nuclear power *and* the peril of the bomb or Chernobyl. We have also the persistence of apartheid presumably due to the intense fear of being engulfed by people or a people.

In this right-wing reaction, both political and religious, there is the possibility of an apparently more controlled, but potentially more destructive way of life. The manifestations of apartheid and above all, perhaps, the Holocaust of the

Jewish people bear a terrible witness to the results of trying to pursue a policy of control. Such is the nature of our conflict over *freedom*. Erich Fromm in *The Fear of Freedom,* written in 1945 yet surely even more relevant now, sums up the process thus:

> Freedom has a two-fold meaning for modern man: that he has been freed from traditional authorities and has become an 'individual', but at the same time he has become isolated, powerless, and an instrument of purposes outside himself, alienated from himself and others; furthermore, that this state undermines his self, weakens and frightens him, and makes him ready for submission to new kinds of bondage. Positive freedom on the other hand is identical with the full realization of the individual's potentialities, together with his ability to live creatively and spontaneously.[17]

I am suggesting that all of us in one form or another are engaged, within ourselves, in this dialogue or conflict between our fear of and longing for freedom. For religious people this will extend to their faith, and may indeed be experienced most acutely when the heart of faith and belief is the issue, just because this area can be the vehicle for our deepest emotional fears. I am wanting to *understand* this rather than take sides, for I believe that understanding may help us in personal faith and doubt and in wider situations when religious debates have become very intense, polarized and entrenched.

I am not, though, writing coldly and objectively from outside, but from within the context of those human beings who feel that in the last analysis the particular 'shape' they have discerned in ultimate reality through the religious tradition is at least going in the right direction. Jewish or Christian, we have a core of adherence to the tradition which keeps us engaged, vitally, with it. For me, I think my heart of faith is the affirmation that somehow, and sometimes against all the odds, reality is ultimately creative, not destructive. The issue of creativity and destructiveness is my 'core', and other questions, vital for others, do not seem so important to me.

If pressed I would say that this is a product of the interaction between my own personal experience, my apprehension of the tradition of the nature of God as seen in Christ and the total context — psychological and sociological — in which I have lived. The precise nature of their interaction is not clear to me and perhaps never will be, but I will attempt an illustration of what I mean in the 'Postscript' that follows this chapter.

A problem arises over the different 'cores' for different people, the differing extent to which they can expand or reduce this core and their differing needs for external confirmation or for life inside the religious bodies. This, make no mistake about it, is a terrible dilemma. In raising the possibility of difference we are faced with the question 'is it not a presumptuous fool who kicks against 2000 or 4000 years of tradition and writing?'. Worse, is it not a profound 'sin', whatever that word means?

The burden of ministry

I have talked of all this in general terms because it affects all of us. But I now want to examine the particular position of ministers. It seems that in many senses they are given the task of 'holding' the dilemma of faith and doubt with and for their congregation, just as on another level the entire religious community may have the role of holding it for a wider society.

I am not saying that this is conscious; in fact consciously there has been a shift away from regarding the minister as special in this or any other field, but *unconsciously* it persists. The minister is to hold and guard the truth, and there is of course much in the biblical tradition to reinforce this idea. It is said of ministers: 'they must hold the mystery of the faith with a clear conscience'[18] and 'guard the truth that has been entrusted to you by the Holy Spirit who dwells within us'.[19]

In the letter to the Colossians we have a great plea to ministers and people alike not to be distracted from belief and devotion to Christ: 'see to it that no one makes a prey of you by philosophy and empty deceit, according to human tradition, according to the elemental spirits of the universe, and not according to Christ.'[20] The fact that this was probably directed at first-century gnosticism, the heresy of the time, in no way diminishes the impact it continues to have on successive generations.

Yet through all this debate runs the haunting refrain of Pilate's question 'What is Truth?'. Bacon in his essay *Of Truth* says, 'What is Truth asked jesting Pilate, and would not stay for an answer'.[21] In fact Jesus gives no answer; Pilate is required to supply his own answer on the evidence he has heard — on the implied claims of Jesus throughout the gospel to have and be Truth. So the question remains. Do we externalize 'Truth' and find it in the life and teaching of Jesus or do we need to react rather differently? Should we not remain faithful to our own truth as Jesus did to his?

In facing this dilemma ministers are in a quite different position to other caring professionals whose role on the whole stops short of explicit exposure and explication of their ultimate belief position. Any professional has values, and it is naive to think that they do not affect his or her work, but usually there is elbow-room for development, doubt, modification and negation. But Christian ministers are committed to the Christian *faith*, Jewish rabbis to the Jewish *faith*; furthermore, both are committed to *expounding and teaching* these very traditions.

In Chapter 7 we shall need to explore further the strains that are engendered by the constant requirement to teach and proclaim, but I want to take time at this point to look more closely at the conflicts that can arise from our need, as ministers, to *be* committed to faith and a relationship to God.

The first point to notice is that in order to become ministers at all, rather than another kind of caring professional, we shall necessarily have a large investment in the dimension of relationship with God. It is possible for this to get obscured by the teaching and proclaiming function, particularly perhaps for Jewish rabbis who stand almost by definition as teachers *par excellence.* It is also possible for it to get obscured by the pastoral function of caring for people. But when the chips are down it must be, I feel, that our faith and belief are primary to any function. Without that conscious point of reference, without some *conscious* sense at some point in our lives of the pull of God on us most of us would never have become ministers. In later years some of us have to admit that there was a lot in it of wanting status, security, power, etc., but that awareness is not often part of our conscious decision in initially offering ourselves.

So, faith and belief are primary, but the last sentence already shows that it is not as simple as just stating that. I have already suggested, in this chapter,[22] a powerful yet obscure connection between the religious dimension of life and strong human feelings, particularly those of a primitive kind originating very early in our lives. I *hope* I have also managed to communicate the affirmation that this is not *all* there is to the religious dimension. But the question inevitably arises as to how far any of our belief systems is the expression of a mature encounter and relationship with the Other, with God, and how far it is the container *and* transmitter of our more primitive and probably more damaged selves.

The need for containment will of course depend on how damaged we are but since none of us can come through our early experience unscathed it is bound to be there to some extent. I do not see it as intrinsically undesirable: containment can give our damage a chance to heal. But the difficulty comes when we are so damaged as to be either inordinately fascinated by the very raw and primitive, and sucked irresistibly and completely into it, or to have the need to keep very high and rigid defences against this whole area from fear of just this engulfment. Furthermore we follow either of these paths very often *unconscious* of what is happening to us.

So we can give ourselves to ministry unconsciously hoping that the necessary ordering of faith and life will somehow domesticate and protect us from the excesses of the wilder dimension that is, unknown to us, inside us. Perhaps it will give us just this protection until and unless other people rock the boat and challenge the boundaries of faith or belief. Then we shall feel the need to defend our position with a force commensurate to the intensity of the threat to our identity that is aroused. Such may be the position of extreme fundamentalists or extreme protagonists in the debates on the ordination of women and homosexuality. If we are that sort of person we cannot afford to be more tolerant; it would be too risky. But let me say here that none of us can throw stones in this area: even if we are not usually given to extremes or fanaticism we can be triggered off if something suddenly touches a particular area in us. When this happens we tend to use any external means we can to back up our position: the most powerful and available are likely to be the biblical tradition and that of the religious group to which we belong. If it seems that our own community is likely to fail us then *in extremis* we are likely to move to another.

The difficulty is that we shall do all this in the name of *conscience* — our ultimate, secret weapon — and for all of us it is hard to sort out when our 'conscience' is the expression of our maturity and when it is the voice of our damaged self. We are likely to have to use the defences of *splitting* and *projecting* to make sure our equilibrium does not get disturbed beyond a point we can tolerate: the other people will have to be 'wrong', and there will be little room for dialogue and negotiation.

Alternatively, we can defend ourselves by *denying* that this continuum of faith, belief and doubt has any importance at all for us. We can do this either by an explicit and direct denial of doubt, or by channelling all energy away from this central area into other highways and byways of ministry. We can therefore become religious bureaucrats, religious philanthropists, rigid ritualists or ineffectual academics, anything so that emotions disturbed by an encounter with Omnipotence and/or Love shall not see the light of day.

Thirdly, we can 'know', even if obscurely, that we are disturbed in this area where religious faith and deeply-buried human emotions correspond and interact. Life in ministry may allow such knowledge to continue being half-conscious and half accessible to us; our belief and practice act as the container. This may, in effect, work rather well *for us,* but can be dangerous for those to whom we minister, to the extent to which we are unconscious of what is happening. For we partly know and partly do not know; we partly recognize reverberations from this area of our being but we have not been able to resolve and integrate them. The part we have not worked through may get pushed out on to other people through the sermons we preach, the books we may write and the pastoral care we engage in. The fuller implications of this for our work of ministry belong to other chapters,[23] but the point I would like to emphasize now is that those most at risk may be those of us with some 'out there' knowledge of psychological processes but no experience of working at them personally in the sort of relationship offered by a therapist or a discerning spiritual director.

We could, if we wanted to, learn much about ourselves

through becoming aware of the fluctuations and vicissitudes of our belief and our spiritual lives. But in fact this area features little in our five case histories. John is asking himself questions about what he believes and is aware of difficulties in his spiritual life, but rather late in the day. Anne is apparently most concerned about her work and her relationships, though we can guess that in the worst of her depression anxieties about religious life and faith itself are present. *Robert* has vague twinges that the liturgy and preaching are going dead on him, but in none of them is the faith dimension presented as a major concern. Yet *I* am now presenting it as a very major issue.

The discrepancy stems, I think, from the very high investment ministers have in this whole area. On one very practical level, difficulties of faith which get out of hand can put us out of a job and leave us without material security. This is actually one very good reason why we may, albeit unconsciously, not allow them to rear their heads.

We may not, though, be able to keep them out — but we then have another device available to us; we can keep them very private and hidden, to be discussed only in retreat or in confession and on no account to be allowed to impinge upon our more total lives. This is a very subtle defence and depends on *splitting.* If we separate and *keep apart* our 'ordinary' and 'spiritual' milieux the connection between our spiritual and emotional lives may be able to stay *repressed.* This is less possible with the advent of intensive, individually directed retreats, and it is not for nothing that participants for the long thirty-day version are quite carefully selected. For under such circumstances it is likely that the spiritual and human *will* connect and some people may not be able to take this; their defences become more rigid and the whole experience becomes less than helpful to them, or they crack psychologically.

The five stories do not include any account of retreats, conversations with directors or the like, so this issue is not featured.

Many ministers feel constrained against acknowledging problems of faith and belief. They are constrained by the expectations of others and by their own inner selves. But if this constraint fails it can fail rather thoroughly as is seen when ministers suddenly decide to share all their questioning — now enlarged to crisis point — with their unsuspecting and bewildered congregation, usually *rationalizing* this by saying that it is 'good' for the congregation to know their minister is human and has doubts. The whole thing then gets out of hand.

I am now impinging on the material of the next chapter, but I want to end this one by emphasizing again both the centrality of the whole dimension of faith and belief for the totality of our being as ministers *and* the need, gradually and consistently, to come to grips with it. For all of us, ministers and lay people alike, our religious belief and practice can either contribute to the healing of our scars and to our growth into mature people, or can serve to hide these scars and allow the wounds that gave rise to them to fester more deeply and more insidiously.

Healing often takes place 'below' the level of rational thought and investigation, and if we dig ourselves up too much to see whether this is happening we may stop the process. But having said this, we all, for our emotional health, need to discern broadly which direction we are going in. For those of us who are ministers I feel that to keep somehow engaged with this task — however difficult it may be, and it *is* difficult — is an essential part of responsibility and accountability in our ministry, and in a strange way a fulfilment of our commission to 'guard the truth'.

Postscript to Chapter 6

I want to attempt to illustrate, by an example of personal thinking, what I mean by the dialogue between the religious tradition, personal experience and more general psychological insights. True to my 'core' of creativity and destructiveness, my efforts centre on redemption and atonement, and writing this now at Easter they are again to the fore.

I start from what may feel like three separate places: first, the Christian tradition that in the cross and resurrection of Christ something fundamental for humanity is resolved in a way that makes a fuller and freer way of being possible for us.

Secondly, I draw on various bits of personal experience

that have allowed me to hope, sometimes against all the odds, that the strongest force is creative and not destructive. 'Against all the odds' includes personal odds *and* the experience of others whose conclusion has had to be that ultimate reality for them is destructive rather than creative. The experience of others has to be included in the same way that we cannot dismiss the despair, defeat and suicide of Judas from the passion narrative. We cannot pick and choose.

Thirdly, I am drawing on a body of psychological thought.[24] I know that in so doing I am violating the complexity of that thought, but I do not really want to apologize since this is not meant to be a textbook either of theology or psychology. I find useful the idea that a significant stage in our human development is reached when we do not have to *split* our positive from our negative feelings and put all our positive, loving feelings on to one person or thing and all our negative, hating feelings on to another person or thing; that is when we can let them come together towards the same person or thing *and* recognize that we are one whole person experiencing all these feelings. This capacity seems to be a foundation point for more adult relationships, and the usual person on whom this is first worked out is mother. We can make this integration only if we feel that neither she nor we are destroyed by our hate or overwhelmed by our guilt, and if the knowledge of both of these creates in us not depression and despair, but possibilities of love and making reparation for our 'bad' aspects. In an earlier stage of development we would have been more likely to feel fear of a kind that could persecute and destroy both us and the other person.

Christianity has claimed to be such a turning-point. All the Easter hymns point to the triumph of love over hate and death; for example:

> Love's redeeming work is done;
> Fought the fight, the battle won:
> Lo, our Sun's eclipse is o'er;
> Lo, he sets in blood no more.[25]

Yet, in many ways, the gospel is presented as a *split* between love and hate, the love of God and the hate of man or the love of Jesus and the hate of *some* men — located in the story in the Jews — and the love of *other* men, located in the story in the disciples. Still, however, the passion of Christ is claimed as *the* turning-point, *the* new way forward. Is this born out by or can it bear out our psychological insights? Can we risk letting the two stories 'talk' to each other to see?

I came to read Sebastian Moore's *The Crucified is no Stranger.*[26] His thesis is that in the passion of Christ the aggression of man is invited to have full rein. I then contrasted to this the usual Holy Week addresses when we are exhorted to identify with the faithful and penitent disciples and occasionally with the central figure, but not with the aggressors, except as a quick reminder of how sinful they and we (humankind) are in bringing about the death of the Lord. Then I began to realize how this protects us from the full impact of our feelings.

Nowhere is this more strong than in the reading of the passion according to St John on Good Friday. Here the *split* is effected and kept up between the 'bad' Jews and the 'good': 'Mary by the cross of Jesus' and others faithful to him. The saving grace seems to me to lie in the reproaches. In responding inwardly to the 'O, my People'[27] we are allowed to identify more with our own hate, in its murderousness and crucifyingness, if only we can let this identification happen.

The Good Friday liturgy can be a tremendous opportunity within the 'safety' of the liturgy to identify with *all* the parts and people in it. Shorn of any addresses we are free to put our identification where we will. Our later history has conditioned us to put it on the 'side' of guilt and love, but in this we lose the opportunity for experiencing and exploring our hate.

For us the anger and hate is directed, perhaps, at a love that makes demands on us, is too perfect and so allows us little room for our imperfections, that disillusions us by not giving us what we want — as the historical Jesus did to the historical Jews when he would not be their king. This is the same anger that we have experienced in relation to other human beings, from our mother on. What an opportunity we miss if when entering into the story of the Passion we split off the hater in us and locate it only in the Jews. We split off, too, the betrayer in us, the betrayer we see in Judas or Peter — I think it matters not which for the issue is the same. In this splitting we forget the earlier point in the narrative when the act of betrayal was accompanied by a kiss, and we forget also the fateful 'the Lord turned and looked on Peter', so reminiscent of the earlier call of God in the garden, 'Adam, where are you?'. In this forgetting we separate ourselves from ourselves and from him. By splitting the Passion story into 'goodies' and 'baddies', by selecting our identifications in the liturgy and not being open to its whole, I think we miss both the totality and immensity of the drama and the inner discovery of what happens to (and what God does with) our hate if we can bear to experience it. So perhaps our hate stays unredeemed. I can echo the dictum of fourth-century Gregory of Nazianzus: 'That which is not assumed is not redeemed'.[28] He was talking of the incarnation of God, but perhaps it can be paraphrased thus and applied to us; 'That which is not recognized and assumed (owned and taken on inside us) cannot be redeemed'. We can thus miss our chance of risking experiencing and expressing our love and hate towards the same person, in this instance towards Christ, or what he stands for, that is God himself.

If we can let the drama unfold in us there is one split, one separation that we cannot avoid, and it is perhaps our intuitive knowledge of this that makes us pale and cut off our participation at an earlier point. This is that separation that Jesus himself experienced, between himself — all humanity — and God when he cries, 'My God, my God, why hast thou forsaken me?'[29] In this he speaks for all of us in our uncertainty as to whether God (or mother) will utterly forsake us if we let rip our hate.

For this reason the 'It is finished'[30] of St John is incomplete and disastrous to us psychologically, even with the better translation, 'It is accomplished'. If the ending or accomplishment of the drama is a death, as in the Greek tragedies with their inexorable fatal playing out of guilt and shame,[31] however profound, inspiring and cathartic that death may be, where will it leave us religiously and psychologically? We will be left with the appalling consequences of our murderous hate; that it is destructive and final. We will be back in the world of the jungle, the world of 'an eye for an eye, a tooth for a tooth', back into the deep fear of our earliest endeavours at human relationship, and left abandoned in a void.

The affirmation of *resurrection* is necessary if we are to be able to believe that love, that God, is not destroyed by hate. The 'It is *accomplished'* of St John points us towards it, but almost in an 'after the event', internal way. I doubt if we could easily affirm it humanly if we did not have the story of the resurrection to validate it for us 'externally', just as it is more difficult for children to believe that their love and hate can be integrated if the actual external death of a parent happens during their development. Perhaps now we can see partly why theological debates on the nature of resurrection cause such anger and anguish. We need it too much.

Yet the different endings to the stories of Judas and Peter show that the death and resurrection process does not work automatically in the life of any individual, however true it may be for the whole race of mankind. Any particular human being, by himself and without help — and even sometimes with it — can go under and be unable to believe that his hate can be contained by love.

The story of Judas allows space for the continuation of tragedy and situations in which love does not seem to triumph. It 'allows' because it is there, not because we can now see our way through that mystery. Suffice it to say here that, though the cross of Christ stands potentially as a resolution of the human conflict between love and hate, it does not *ensure* that this resolution will be effected in every human being. Sometimes the odds seem too great. This is a sobering thought but it will not just go away because we wish it would.

It seems to me that what the Christian story of redemption is offering is an insight that very much corresponds to the psychological story of human experience. In a strange way the two validate each other. Yet there is a conflict. I have suggested a *correspondence* between the two stories. But the traditional doctrines of atonement and the uniqueness of Christ have claimed more than correspondence; they have claimed a *causality* for the Christian story, in proclaiming that in that event our human condition is changed.[32] And psychologically we *are* saying that something is changed in our human development when love and hate come together. I am aware that to some this last will seem far less than the truth, but to others it can pave the way towards the internalization of that which could have remained external, and so be a way into apprehending truth.

I would like to end this postscript with a personal memory which may perhaps illustrate and 'earth' my reflection.

The memory is of Jerusalem at Eastertime. Jerusalem, the shrine of three of the world's great religions, claimed, sometimes exclusively, by each of them. I wandered in the Christian holy places, and in a strange way, apart from the Garden of Gethsemane and the Church of All Nations beside it, they spoke very little to me. I was not quite sure why, but I think it was partly the uncertainty over historicity. It seemed impossible to locate the scene of redemption in the present-day Church of the Holy Sepulchre, and if I did what would it do for me? Would it add anything to or detract from that event as I and others have *internalized* it? Also, in some strange sense, Jerusalem has 'moved on'; she seemed not to belong to me in the sense of being available for an exclusively Christian meditation and experience.

Then I visited *Yad Vashem,* the memorial to the Holocaust in which six million Jews died in Hitler's Europe. By a strange irony it is set on a hill just outside the modern city of Jerusalem. As it happened, because of a personal experience I came to that visit aware and afraid of a potentially destructive conflict inside myself between loving and hating; I came exposed and open to the redemption scenario and story. At that moment, looking at the memorial from Dachau depicting the torture of men by other men, I felt that here was the real Golgotha. Likewise, in the garden on another part of the hill, dedicated to the memory of the children who had died, I had a momentary sense of the tomb and garden of the resurrection.

Was I, in that reverie, doing violence either to the Christian faith or to the Jewish people's sense of outrage when we 'Christianize' their experience? Or was I, as I like to think, in 'moving' the geographical sites, also moving round *inside me* the internal site of all I have taken in about redemption from experience and the Church's tradition — moving round too the roles of victim and persecutor — in the hope that what I have believed about redemption could somehow remain a living reality?

I do not know; I do not know either if my hope is and can

be justified. The point I am wanting to make is that the *hope* of redemption became timeless and internal; even though brought into conscious awareness on that occasion by the events of two thousand years ago, it was no longer completely bounded by those events. The interaction of personal experience, human history and, for me, my Christian experience, became focused on the embers of Auschwitz and the searing question of whether the hate of Auschwitz is the last word of humanity to itself — and somehow and haltingly love flickered back into life.

Notes

1. John Donne, *Nativitie, La Corona,* 3, Divine poems, in John Hayward ed. *John Donne,* Penguin Poets, Penguin 1950.
2. See the image of the garden which both contains love and lets it blossom. Song of Solomon 5.1.
3. Job 38.1; 40.10.
4. Job 42.6.
5. John 14.9.
6. A. M. Ramsey *God, Christ and the World,* SCM 1969, ch. 2.
7. John 1.1.
8. Exodus 33.20.
9. Exodus 19.9; pillars of fire and smoke, Exodus 13.21.
10. Genesis 3.3—4.
11. Genesis 3.9.
12. St Augustine *On Marriage and Desire,* 2.57; *Encheiridion (Handbook of the Christian Religion),* 27.
13. St Irenaeus *Against all Heresies,* 4.37; *Demonstration of the Apostolic Preaching,* 12.
14. David Jenkins, particularly when Bishop Designate of Durham, 1984.
15. *Church Times,* 27 June 1986 and 20 February 1987.
16. D. E. Jenkins *Guide to the Debate about God,* Lutterworth 1966, p. 92.
17. E. Fromm *The Fear of Freedom* Routledge and Kegan Paul 1942, p. 233.
18. 1 Timothy 3.9.
19. 2 Timothy 1.14.
20. Colossians 2.8.
21. Sir Francis Bacon, ed. M. Kiernan *The Essays and Counsels, Civil and Moral,* No. 1: *Of Truth,* Oxford University Press 1985.
22. See pp. 104—5.
23. Especially Chapter 7, pp. 127—9; ch. 10, pp. 201—2.

24. The 'depressive position' — hypothesized stage of childhood development of becoming able to relate with love *and* hate to the same *whole* 'object' (person) and in this developing a capacity for concern and reparative activity — first conceptualized by Melanie Klein and then developed by others within and beyond her immediate group, such as Donald Winnicott. References and further reading: M. Klein, ed. Juliet Mitchell *The Selected Melanie Klein*, Penguin 1986; H. Segal *Melanie Klein* Fontana 1979, ch. 7, 'The Depressive Position'; D. E. Winnicott *Human Nature*, Free Association Books 1988, Part III, ch. 1; or for a summary see N. Symington *The Analytic Experience*, Free Association Books 1986, section on 'Deeper Understanding'.
25. English Hymnal No. 135.
26. S. Moore *The Crucified is no Stranger*, Darton Longman & Todd 1977.
27. Good Friday liturgy, the reproaches: 'O, my People, what have I done unto thee and wherein have I wearied thee? Testify against me.'
28. Gregory of Nazianzus, Ep. 101.7.
29. Mark 15.34.
30. John 19.30.
31. See G. Murray *Aeschylus, the Creator of Tragedy*, Greenwood Press 1978.
32. The theories of Christ as victor, victim and giver of life; see also F. W. Dillistone *Christian Understanding of Atonement*, James Nisbet 1968.

SEVEN

The Strain of Proclaiming

Having attempted in the last chapter to explore the strain to ministers of *being* people of faith and belief we turn now to the other side of that coin. Inherent in the ministerial role, for ministers of all traditions, is the obligation not only to have faith but to communicate it to others by regular preaching, teaching and public prayer. The sources of stress in this are numerous.

The first comes from being required to communicate on such deep and personal issues frequently and regularly. We saw something of this in *John*'s struggles with his Trinity Sunday sermon. Of course many of us know the discipline of constant preparation and presentation; it is something to which teachers in schools and universities are subject all the time, and they too have to stay freshly involved with their material if their communication is to have vitality. Ministers share in this but are subject to something more by virtue of the very nature of the raw material with which we are dealing. To preach can and perhaps should be emotionally demanding. But if it is then to do it week in and week out will impose a strain, particularly if we feel it to be something for which we lack any natural aptitude, and therefore approach with trepidation. An additional hazard is that it is so very public, and many people are anxious about public speaking. Yet in some religious bodies, notably the nonconformist churches, the evangelical wing of the Church of England and the Jewish communities, a minister can be labelled 'good' or 'bad' by the presence or absence of this skill.

Here something less conscious begins to creep in. Many ministers could profitably use some help in the sheer technique of delivering sermons and speaking in public. To some limited extent this *is* provided in theological college, but following ordination and some years' experience it is somehow hard to ask for it. This may be partly because we have a reluctance to admit we need help in this or any other area. Somehow the ingredients of ministry 'should' come to us as easily as falling off a log, and particularly this one for we would not like to think, at least consciously, that we are anxious about a 'performance', for surely the acts of preaching and praying are not meant to be that? Put starkly like this they aren't, yet on another level when we preach, teach or pray in public we *are* being asked to set ourselves forward and 'perform'. In other walks of life it is known and accepted that this 'one person out in front' situation is stressful, even if more so for certain people than others.

I put these two points first because in one sense they are obvious; yet somehow they get missed and some strain which could be relatively easily removed or at least ameliorated is allowed to build up.

Then there arise times when we know quite consciously what we want to say, and realize, also quite consciously, that we are not going to be popular when we say it. The tension becomes prominent when the situation is rather extreme, as in Ireland or South Africa, but it is there at times for most of us, and has been so since biblical times.

In the biblical tradition this is seen most strongly in the prophets who often struggled to stay faithful to the word of God *as they saw it,* when pressed by people to say other things. We have only to think of the false prophets who cried '"Peace, peace," when there is no peace',[1] Nathan's need to face the wrath of the anointed King David in the face of his rebuke over Uriah the Hittite,[2] or Jeremiah who really went through it by insisting on prophesying the fall of Jerusalem when others preferred that he should not do so.[3] We see it in Christ who incurred the terrible wrath of all about him by faithfully proclaiming his 'Father's business' and the truth about himself and others as he was convinced of it.

We may say that this problem comes with the job and that this sort of integrity is what is expected of ministers, but to say this does not necessarily enable it to come easily to us. Yet it is one of the areas in which ministers tend to have high expectations of themselves and upbraid themselves very severely when they feel they fail.

There is a still deeper layer of difficulty and stress which follows almost directly from the content of the last chapter. As ministers we live within a tradition of faith and belief, yet we cannot, if we are alive and vibrant, but have our own internal dialogue with that tradition which may lead us, as it does other people, in and out of 'orthodoxy' and in and out of the dilemma I have already suggested[4] exists in the search for truth. New insights may seem at variance with the tradition as we originally heard it, and as our congregations want it to be proclaimed. The conflict between personal integrity and expectation then takes on a new form which can be relentlessly stressful for the individual minister when integrity becomes an inner need to follow a path of questioning and development. The conflict is centered on how far this can and should be shared with the congregation and/or the wider Church.

On one level it is impossible for the conflict not to be passed on; few of us are as aware and as discerning as to know at any and every point how much of what we are saying in a sermon is turned outwardly towards other people, and how much is an externalization and working out of things inside the self.

Indeed it seems to me that it is right and necessary that we are not always able to make the distinction. For teaching, preaching and all forms of communication that are devoid of personal passion become too cerebral and ultimately irrelevant. But if we are in the midst of a personal belief or spirituality crisis we may find the need to communicate via sermons and prayers on a regular and required basis continuously stressful, even though we may succeed in hiding our discomfort. If there emerges too great a discrepancy between what our being wants to say and what other people want to hear then something is likely to snap — either our health or the relationship between us and our congregation.

I am not here ignoring the responsibility of the other people involved, whether they be parishioners or the wider community, to grow and mature in life and faith and not demand that a minister of religion should always meet them where they are and not where he or she is. But knowing this will not mean that we shall not feel strained by the situation.

What *we* may experience is an ever-increasing sense of exhaustion. What *others* may then notice is a certain staleness in the preaching that is offered and a readiness to do anything else other than preach — read poetry, use the visual arts, have music or dancing instead of a sermon — anything rather than be exposed to the bankruptcy of no longer being able to preach and communicate creatively.

The issue of the relationship between our own inner dialogue and its externalization in teaching and preaching has other facets, some more obvious than others. I would like to spell out in more detail some of those that I see. I then leave it to the reader to protest and say I have made them up, or to react with a sigh of relief that the experience has something in common with their own. Sharing leading to greater understanding is one way of easing strain, but for this to happen there must first be recognition.

Much of what now follows builds upon Chapter 6 but that was, as it were, using a broad brush to try to portray a whole landscape. I want now to concentrate on the details of more circumscribed areas. The first of these is preaching.

The activity of preaching

On one level we preach primarily to ourselves, because in preaching we have an opportunity for externalizing and working on the inner dialogue that is going on inside ourselves. I used to be able to discover my inner preoccupations long before I became really aware of them just by noticing the titles and themes of my sermons, and this was at one and the same time both enlightening and frightening. Enlightening because it helped me know what was going on in me, and frightening because it implied that my congregation was being subjected to a half-digested process which was not at all objective, and may in fact have been unconscious.

This thought can certainly produce a doubt in us as to whose gospel we are proclaiming, and I have already hinted at part of the danger of this and want to expand on it in a later chapter.[5] The issue is this: Do we transmit a healthy part of our unconscious, or a damaged part which can make the whole process destructive? We are, in fact, less likely to do the latter if we can ask the question of ourselves, 'Whose gospel?'. But we cannot halt the emergence and transmission of our unconscious selves unless we are dead inside. To preach from externalities or things we are sure of, or think we are, is no guarantee that our unconscious is not involved *and* calls a halt also to creativity, producing a sort of lifelessness in our material which will certainly communicate itself to those who have to listen.

The problem is not all ours; part of it lies in the 'flip' side of the process. Those who listen get conditioned to accepting our offerings not as something relative and provisional but as an exposition of truth. Of course sophisticated congregations will deny this and say that they are not listening in this way; they are too 'grown-up' to do this. Yet the situation of one person standing up and addressing others must, I feel, reproduce, even if unconsciously, some sort of authority situation or memory, be it of school or of parents — and the inner reaction sometimes fits this earlier situation better than it does the current 'adult' one.

To give a personal example of this sort of hazard: I used to get quite confused and disconsolate about the mixed reactions my sermon efforts aroused. I was not aware enough to know that in my sermons I sometimes touched, quite unconsciously, deep material about fears of non-existence, or being destroyed by anger that aroused equally unconscious reactions in those who heard me. When they reacted with anger I was disturbed. And it is still difficult to ascertain whether I was preaching from somewhere disturbed in me, or whether I was in fact quite 'together', but the whole sermon context roused the vulnerabilities of those who heard me.

The process of unconscious interplay is an ever-present hazard rumbling on, as it were, in the background. The foreground contains a different dimension: we need, when preaching, to take *consciously* into our own inner dialogue the encounter with those we are preaching to. What we say is going to be coloured by our appreciation of the situation and, if we are preaching to the same group of people regularly, by our more total involvement in the life of the group. For this reason a 'one-off' sermon to a group we do not know may be both more and less difficult than preaching to the same group of people all the time. It is more difficult because there is little to engage with; we have to fall back on our *stereotypes*[6] of what this particular congregation is likely to be like, and because this is a surface impression we may in fact completely miss the mark, unless we can somehow 'tune in' deeper as we go along. Because we do not know anyone intimately we inevitably address our perception of that group and our own reasons as to why they might have come together. For example, an invitation to address a large cathedral congregation feels very different from one to address a smaller group of people who meet regularly on an informal level. We bring to the former presumptions of desired anonymity, formality, non-intimacy, and to the latter a desire for sharing and the more personal. We may be right in our presuppositions or we may be wrong. It is difficult to know; the style of address which is likely truly to communicate to these congregations is bound to be different, that we can see, but whether our perception of the difference fits the reality is another matter, and the situation is more 'hit and miss' than we would wish. So too in the formidable task of addressing an unknown group in a human crisis such as a funeral. We have to start with our perception of what this occasion is likely to mean to the people concerned; this will get modified by whatever actual knowledge of any of the people we have or can get. But inevitably there will remain a gap between perception and knowledge and this will get filled by our own personal experience of what this sort of occasion could mean or has meant to us. Unless we are to preach a totally uninspiring sermon it is on this personal experience that we shall have to draw, whether we are aware of it or not, and risk its hazards.

Preaching continuously to a congregation we know well contains a different hazard, that of being very involved in the life of the community. This gets reflected in comments such as 'didn't you think the vicar was rather getting at us in his sermon today?' or 'perhaps the vicar is having rows with his wife from the way he was preaching?'. This can be extremely unnerving to a preacher, for it makes us feel very exposed.

There are likely, too, to be mismatches in the purpose of a sermon or address. When I was first learning to preach somebody whose opinion I valued said, 'You should offer before you demand'. This makes sound sense for it is of the essence of good practice in other human relationship fields. A counselling supervisor who first tells a student all that is wrong with his work and demands that he does better is likely to induce a paralysis in listening and commitment through a reaction of resentment. A tutor who cannot give something of his own enthusiasm to his pupil is unlikely to make much progress. In the same way preaching requires a generosity in us.

But what if on a certain subject we feel that we have nothing to give and only questions to raise? Maybe we can do no other than follow through our inner state, but we should not be surprised if this arouses opposition in those who come to listen to us. Understanding that we have demanded effort without giving anything, even if we could not help doing so, can reduce the disturbance in us. The position, however, gets more complicated than this! Whether we proclaim and give or meditate a question aloud is likely to have a different effect on different people in the congregation, according to the state of *their* internal dialogue. I took on board my colleague's comment about offering before demanding; what it took me a lot longer to understand was that what is offering to one person feels like demanding to another.

For some people a sermon that opens up questions rather than gives definitive answers allows the heart and mind to expand and is experienced like a breath of fresh air creating a valued and contained space for inner exploration. This sort of person is likely to feel trapped in a presentation that has tight boundaries with no rough edges: he or she feels rebellious and wants to kick at it. Their need at that point is for inner freedom and space and it is this that feels safe; indeed, it is a gift. For other people the exact reverse is true. Open-endedness is demanding and produces an alarming degreee of anxiety. These people desire to be given finite and definite boundaries. If these are there then they can explore inside them; if they are not they will feel unsafe and angry at the source of their anxiety, in this instance the preacher. So it is impossible to please everyone, but some awareness of why we sometimes get the reaction we do to what we say can reduce our own sense of puzzlement and disquiet.

Preaching is one dimension of proclaiming that can be more complicated and hazardous than might at first appear. But there is another very general issue that extends to all forms of communication and this has to do with the different ways in which people *think*. In particular, at this point I am wanting to explore the difference between concrete and symbolic thinking.

Concrete and symbolic thinking

Most people, either permanently or at different stages in their lives, tend to think either concretely and literally or symbolically. Consider, for example, a red rose. To a person who thinks concretely a red rose means a red flower that blooms in summer and grows on a bush with thorns on it. That will be all there is to it. To a person who thinks symbolically a red rose symbolizes or 'stands for' beauty, a token of love or even a drop of blood, and indeed this is the way that it has been depicted in poetry.

These two sorts of people do not understand each other very well but a minister will meet both and is supposed to understand both. This is going to be difficult and a strain.

To think concretely or symbolically can be a matter of intellectual level *or* a product of emotional development. Where it is the former the discrepancy between the two sorts of people is not likely to disappear, and a minister has the task of containing, forever, both of them within the same congregation. Because of the communication gap conflicts and controversies erupt, for example on whether an empty tomb is a necessary prerequisite of resurrection, or whether a virgin birth is necessary to the process of incarnation. To someone who thinks literally and concretely the resurrection of Christ presupposes a lack of a corpse and therefore an empty tomb, and to see Jesus as the Son of God requires a virgin birth. To those who think symbolically the processes of resurrection and incarnation are more internal, and they will not be so bothered by the historical question and irritated by those who are.

Difficulties in belief are also going to differ. A literal thinker's faith is going to be disrupted if the history can be shown to be false or in doubt; a symbolic thinker's faith can develop relatively undisturbed by that but gets disturbed by feeling trapped in a demand for assent to historical truth. At one end of the continuum are those, like Bultmann, who can maintain that the impact of death and resurrection would stand even if the whole life of Jesus was shown to be mythological;[7] at the other end are those for whom the whole of faith is threatened if one part of the historical infrastructure fails or is thought to fail. Difficulties in this area have not been confined to the issues of resurrection and incarnation, but over the years have become focused in interpretations of more discrete issues such as the sexuality of Jesus.

Where the difference between people is not one of difference in basic intellectual style but more mediated by emotional causes and conditions the problem is no less acute, though there may be more possibility of change and flexibility. But it is a source of strain for ministers when either their basic style does not coincide with that of their congregations, or when their or their congregation's emotional position is hampering development and mutual understanding.

One thing we cannot do, either to ourselves or to others, is to force a particular kind of belief on those who cannot believe in this way; at least not without doing violence to them. Yet a great deal of violence, mostly, in this day and age, non-physical, has been perpetrated in the name of enforcing a 'right' way of thinking or belief. That fact alone might make us stop and think as to whether we can possibly be right to exact it. If we think 'no' we have a problem of how to contain these very different views, and I do not have any easy answer to this. For I am aware of the danger of so fudging and blurring all boundaries that identity is lost and all is chaos, yet also of the strain of feeling so trapped as not to be able to 'breathe'.

For those who think literally the strain comes when thought or events seem to threaten their literal holding on certain facts. They *feel* they need a certain form of faith, and that they are being asked to *believe* that they don't. So a sort of inner war starts, sometimes ending by taking up an even more entrenched position, or paradoxically by a total loss of faith. We see this latter in the phenomenon of people converted to a fundamentalist faith who completely lose faith some years later. The strain is in accommodating any development in external thought; it cannot enter into dialogue with the internal emotional world of that person, and so feels very intrusive and threatening.

For the symbolic thinker the strain is almost the opposite. Belief is internalized anyway in symbols; there is no problem about starting a dialogue between internal and external worlds; the situation is fluid — too fluid for comfort. Symbols that were alive can go dead and require rebirth or transformation, which can mean periods in darkness and doubt with little to draw on in the way of help, though the experience and example of others who have been on a similar path offer 'crumbs'.

For both kinds of person the boundaries of their being can be challenged in ways that feel extremely uncomfortable. What often happens is that each kind looks for support in talking to and mixing with those of a similar 'persuasion', thus often perpetuating factions and *splits* in communities of faith. The spoken or unspoken question is the desperate 'are you with us or against us?', *not* 'can we together get some light on what's going on?'.

I would emphasize here that this sort of process *hurts.* Each kind of person can be really bothered by even the continued presence of the other. It is inevitable that from time to time peaceful coexistence will give way to open confusion, disturbance and even apparent warfare. In this climate the wear and tear on ministers can be very high.

First, we have our own personal place in this arena, our own personal defences of that place and our own personal escape routes if the going gets too tough. But our personal process has to meet and interact with that of those to whom we minister. If they tend to think mostly the same way as we do the strain is mitigated somewhat, but if they are varied in their approach, or we have to relate to many groups and congregations, as do the bishops, the resulting stress can feel colossal. The temptation then is to retreat into an entrenched position or to sell out to being tossed around by controversy, and neither of these is likely to do a lot for our emotional well-being.

This whole issue is one of how to contain and value *difference,* but the last area I want to explore in this chapter is almost the opposite, that of being *inclusive.* We have to confront this in many guises, but there are a cluster that merit particular exploration here, namely inclusive language, liturgy and experience.

Inclusive language, liturgy and experience

Inclusive language

Current controversy on the role of women has led many to question the masculine language we have traditionally used both for God and in our general talk of human beings, which is seen as exclusive and oppressive. I am probably guilty of it in what I have written, and I both apologize and do not apologize.

I apologize because I have succumbed to the limiting power of language; any language does constrain our thoughts and feelings. But to communicate at all in an adult way we need language, and a struggle to be consciously inclusive all the time often restricts a free flow of ideas and words. Not to be inclusive, however, may seriously offend people and so render them quite incapable of really listening to what we want to say.

The subject generates a lot of heat and even disbelief: 'Can you *really* not bear God to be addressed as "Father"'; 'Aren't you really making a bit too much fuss over quite a little thing?'. I want to say that it is not a small thing because our use of language reflects our internal state and so does our 'rebellion' against any language.

If, internally, we feel deprived of something of motherhood in using 'father' for God then we are going to be angry and revolt. If we feel it perpetuates an oppression of women in our total community we are also going to be hurt and angry. But if we let the debate rest there and do not go on to ask the question 'why has this debate become so entrenched and some people so *for* change and others so *against* it?' then I think we miss the chance of a deeper understanding of the problem.

Whatever may seem to be the 'top level', conscious situation, there is another layer of which some people, through their personal history, have been made conscious and others have not. This other layer is the opposite of oppression of women; it is the *power* of women which each of us has experienced in our relationship with our mothers. That first relationship, above all, involved dependence and I have already said enough earlier[8] to indicate that a position of dependence on another human being can be very disturbing and painful to us. So our fear may well be of the power we might be letting loose if we incorporate the 'she' into our religious language and, above all, use the 'she' to talk of God, or include the 'she' by our use of inclusive terms. This may help to shed some light on the intensity of the controversy over the ordination of women to the priesthood, though I am aware that what I am about to say represents a tentative and necessarily speculative exploration of the issue.

It is my impression that opposition to the ordination of women comes from two subgroups within the churches. The first group consists of the more biblically-oriented 'lower' churches who cite the biblical evidence for non-ordination, maintaining that the whole stability of the natural and supernatural 'order of things' would be endangered if power and authority did not remain with men.

The second source of opposition is those religious traditions in which the Eucharist is central and the symbolic role of the minister most important. Here I think we are dealing with the inclusion, or intrusion, of sexuality into the liturgy. And not only adult sexuality but reverberations and half-remembrances of all our childhoods in which the power of mother was paramount, even if at times hidden from us. This is a huge subject and I cannot do justice to it here, but I am suggesting that the fantasy of women presidents at the Eucharist can be so frightening and unwelcome because it raises unconsciously such issues as the power of woman/mother to nourish or deprive us, the sexual jealousies and rivalries between adult men and women and our forgotten memories of coming out of the world of mother into one where we had to relate to different sorts of people. An all-male priesthood allows us to rest from dealing with these issues, and saves us from disturbance and confusion.

Such may be our disturbing *fantasies,* which have invested the debate with such intensity. But it is also my impression that on the whole the *reality* is different. Women ministers do not seem so far to have thrown the whole thing out of control and into chaos; where there are women priests we do not seem to have been overwhelmed by primitive emotions, though more adult areas of jealousy and competition do seem sometimes to have been roused. But I am not sure that we shall get further into resolving this very difficult area, except by continuing to risk a progressive testing of reality and by attempting to explore and understand what could be going on in the depths concerning this issue and debate. It seems to me that here, above all, the theological dimension is being asked to bear a load extra and above its 'proper' sphere, and this extra is the contribution of the story of human development.

Inclusive liturgy

It is not only the issue of inclusive language involving the sexes that taps into deeper emotional factors of human development. A similar process happens with any linguistic reform of the liturgy, sharpened by the fact that the liturgy is public and has to serve the needs of many people. For example, our attitude to the inclusion or exclusion of the 'cursing psalms'[9] may be much more intimately connected to our emotional handling of anger and hatred than we would care to admit. We have also the great lovers and haters of the 1662 *Book of Common Prayer* or the Latin Mass. To reject Cranmer's English or the Latin Mass on the grounds that they are incomprehensible and irrelevant to many of those who come to the liturgy is certainly a very valid *external* point, but I have a sense that for some of us Cranmer's English, like Shakespeare's, reaches an inarticulate inner level of our being, and that we therefore react emotionally and sometimes in what seems a very irrational way. This is a far cry from the intellectual judgement of irrelevancy, but unless we take it into account something in liturgical reform won't go 'quite right'.

The problem for those of us who have to preach and communicate is that there does not seem an easy solution. To remake the liturgy for the particular worshipping group is unrealistic and probably destructive of a sense of togetherness within the religious communities. Some people would not mind this, but others would, feeling a deep loss and sense of fragmentation just below the surface of things. A lowest common denominator language and liturgy rarely satisfies anyone; it becomes monochrome and domesticated and cannot be a vehicle for the limitless realities that the liturgy is trying to address.

The only way through may be to admit that we cannot get it right and to try to use the controversies about language and liturgy to increase our conscious awareness of the emotional issues that are around. A sermon trying to understand what underlies the problem of inclusive language might be of more help and value than one that painstakingly tries to use it all the time! The other thing that can help is to face our objections to the language that is being used, to the bits of the liturgy that are or are not being omitted, and sometimes to subject ourselves to an approach with which we are not emotionally comfortable, and try to discover on a deeper level why this is so. Herein lies the value of the tradition: it allows us a framework for exploration in order to decrease our internal defences and increase our internal freedom.

But all this is hard for ministers; we are required to provide a liturgy that is satisfying and to deal with our own and other people's inner reaction to it at one and the same time. It is made still more complicated when we come up against more apparently irrational things; the congregation, or ourselves, are inordinately attached to a particular hymn tune; here it is the non-verbal that is operating. How often have we heard people say with quite intense disappointment, 'It was my favourite hymn, but the wrong tune'? The sense is of a quite big deprivation. This raises the whole question as to whether religious faith and practice can make up to us for our emotional gaps and difficulties; rather surprisingly to myself I have come to it through the issue of language and liturgy.

Inclusive experience

To avoid misunderstanding and the writing off of what I want to explore let me emphasize that I am accepting that on the external level we need to address ourselves to ameliorating the difficulties caused by forms of language and liturgy. But on another level I am wondering whether our plea for inclusive language and liturgy is masking a deeper, more hidden plea for an *inclusive experience,* most probably of understanding and love. And that when the external form fails us our anger at this is tapping into a layer of anger of when experience has failed us.

Perhaps I may illustrate what I mean by a personal

example. I was long puzzled and rather upset by the sense that at Eastertide I never seemed to get beyond Good Friday or possibly Easter Eve; language and the liturgy went dead from then on. I paid lip-service to Easter joy; I had to because I couldn't escape it and had to preach it, but it never meant much to me internally. It took me a long time to realize that I had never come to terms with certain losses in my personal life which, when they occurred, felt like death. I realized that if my mourning for them is not really accomplished then it is not so surprising that I am unable to tune in fully to the experience of the overcoming of death that the Christian faith proclaims. The liturgy cannot 'make it up' to me. That does not invalidate the tradition; in fact it was the tradition that alerted me to the emotional problem. But once I began to recognize and accept the way things were, I began to feel less strained, less out on a limb, less guilty about my apparent deficiency, and less caught up in a frenzied effort to remedy the state of affairs.

The general issue for us here is the one we have already encountered[10] when we talked of relationship with God, and ministry containing and healing our more damaged selves. We have to confront the question as to whether we can find in the love of God something to make up for us what we have lacked in human love. Such is of course the implied claim of religious experience, seen most clearly perhaps in the 'conversion' experience, but I have to admit great doubt here, for it is not certainly so. In and amongst all the people who have found love and fulfilment through their religious faith and practice there are those who have felt ultimately forced to turn away from it, sometimes in a sense of hate and outrage. We have probably also all of us known religious people who have become bitter and disillusioned, and those who after a life of commitment die in seeming despair. This we cannot gainsay and it poses a very disturbing question: Did people's practice of faith somehow fail or were their expectations of it too great? For those in ministry it is certainly not an academic question. We usually do not know all of why we have become ministers, but if there has been *an* element in it of wanting to make up for something we have not had humanly, *can* ministry, or even faith and belief itself, do this for us, and how shall we feel if it seems that it cannot?

Religious faith alone, without an attempt to work through and become conscious of the human factors involved, will not hold some of us. I do not want to say that it will not hold others — that would be to deny their experience. Neither do I want to say that belief and practice are, *per se,* defence against our humanness. They *may* be, and I think have been for me at times, but I cannot lay down the law and will not close the question. Even if they are sometimes a defence, for many of us they may, for much of the time, be a 'good enough' defence, and like 'good enough' mothering be sufficient to allow us to grow. For it is a mistake to think that we can grow in total nakedness.

Those of us who do feel the need to ask and struggle with this question may be doing something important *or* unbelievably arrogant, and I do not see that we can easily know which. All we can ask of each other is a certain tolerance. This is hard to grant, as past and present history of persecution of unbelievers and doubters has shown, perhaps because the question 'Can faith deliver the goods?' is so important to us. This question is a source of strain for us and we do not talk enough about it.

The task of continuing proclaiming *and* believing in and amongst all these issues is hard, and from at least Moses and Jeremiah onwards has caused a good deal of suffering for the individuals concerned. Some of the strain is endemic to the situation and cannot be taken away, but it can be mitigated and relieved if we can take time to talk about it and try to recognize and understand some of its more hidden ingredients.

Notes

1. Jeremiah 6.14.
2. 2 Samuel 12.7ff.
3. Jeremiah 26.
4. See ch. 6, pp. 107—9.
5. *The dangers of being unaware*: see ch. 6, pp. 113—14, and ch. 10, pp. 201—2.
6. *Stereotypes*: see ch. 3, pp. 62—4.

7. Rudolf Bultmann *Essays I: The Crisis in Belief,* SCM 1955.
8. *Dependence*: see ch. 5, pp. 99–102 and ch. 6, pp. 104ff.
9. e.g. Psalm 137, vv. 8, 9, Psalm 58.
10. *Religion the vehicle of our damaged selves*: see ch. 6, pp. 112ff.

EIGHT

The Strain of 'Being'

In contrast to the theme of Chapters 6 and 7, the strain associated with *being* a minister has received a considerable amount of overt attention. We have already noted in earlier chapters[1] the sorts of impossible things demanded and expected of ministers, together with the various attempts that have been made to ameliorate this situation. We saw also the high price that is exacted for failure to meet the ideal, in terms of the condemnation and punitive behaviour of others.

In this chapter I want to look in more detail at the areas of our being in which, as ministers, we are most likely to experience pressure and expectation, either from ourselves or from others.

We need, I think, first to look at one unpalatable possibility, namely that the pressures are *not* really that great and in any case no greater than those which assail others in comparable positions of community leadership, but that those of us who are and have been in ministry do not cope very well with this sort of pressure. I have to say that I think there may be some truth in this, stemming from the personalities and defence systems of those of us who offer ourselves to this way of life. We can speculate on the differences between Robert, of our five case studies, and his brother, the successful city stockbroker. Robert, in his soliloquy, clearly despises the rat-race world of his brother, but is this partly a defence against an inability in him to begin to compete in it?

Of course, on the one hand, this quality is not necessarily negative. We may have real reservations about wanting or achieving the competitiveness, apparent ruthlessness, and inevitable stress-levels of the executive life. But we may also have to admit that, until comparatively recently, being a minister could be a slightly protected way of life. Once

141

ordained and licensed — provided we did not commit gross sins — living and housing were secure even if preferment did not come very easily. Even that was 'all right', since ministers should not really have promotion ambitions — as Robert is maintaining. Similarly, once elected to profession in a religious community life could be expected to be materially secure. Overall, the level of security varied, the Anglican system of freehold being perhaps the most secure, and the Free Church and Jewish systems less secure, with more possibility of moves and more need to prove oneself and be accountable to the congregation. But, generally speaking, we, as ministers, were not perhaps very accustomed to the 'toughness' that many other people have to face in their careers.

Be that as it may, developments in systems of accountability and the limiting of the parson's freehold have met with suspicion and hostility. They go against the grain of what we may have been led to expect. What is more, there rises the protest, and this not only from ministers, but also from those of us who work in such other caring institutions as the NHS, 'we work with people, and we cannot put that work into the strait-jacket of a business-like evaluation process'. There is of course truth in this, but I have a sneaking sense that those of us in the caring professions may, at some unacknowledged level of our being, have gone into this sort of work hoping that it never could be evaluated and we could therefore never be found really wanting. What we miss sight of is that without some sort of evaluation we cannot really see our achievements easily either. The lack of evaluation may apparently protect the more vulnerable aspects of our self-esteem, but the potential for *developing* self-esteem through a sensitive and supportive evaluation process is also lost.

Being a minister or Religious can also seem automatically to confer a status on the person which he or she might not easily have acquired otherwise. It can provide a safe sanctuary or 'raised ground' away from some areas of our humanness, for example sexuality. If the sense of status breaks down then the minister may find a new role, picked up in caricature by various TV series: that of the amiable, even lovable 'clown', who can get away with not being very efficient, not being very good at the job, and whose harassment by all and sundry is the subject of much mirth. But in reality the 'self' living underneath a vocation to ministry may be rather frail and vulnerable, not able to stand up very well to criticism if it is justified, or to attack, if not.

Such people tend to be very defended, as Robert is, though we saw that he cannot keep his defences up all the time; they tend to crumble when he is forced to look at how things are going. It is hard for them to admit anxiety, depression, deprivation, anger, resentment at a low salary or almost any other feeling, for to let such feelings in might overwhelm them. And so it is just these sorts of feelings that can be *projected* out on to the congregation and others to the ultimate detriment of all. This all connects strongly with the issue of *inclusive experience* that emerged in Chapter 7[2] and the question of whether the religious dimension of life, and, *a fortiori,* being a minister, contains and then challenges our damaged selves, thus facilitating healing and growth, or whether it reinforces only the damaged part.

To me, it is not self-evident which way the argument will go; I have already talked of both the reassuring and the threatening aspects of the figure of Christ,[3] but it is also true that sustained meditation upon his life and teaching can allow a partial identification with him and so a taking in of something good that can be a real and true foundation for increased inner strength *and* increased capacity for self-awareness and the ability to bear emotional reality. Moreover, encounter with the essential *unknownness* of God has the potential to become the vehicle by which we come to shed, progressively, our various idolatries, human and religious, and plumb exciting depths which are subversive to any 'cosy' way of being. But I think that most of us need the help of another human person in this process, a theme to which I shall return in the final chapter.[4]

I have put this aspect of things first because I think it needs to be said and admitted, not because I think that it is the whole story. But it is an aspect probably shared by all those who go into work or professions that give them some sort of 'persona', or mask. Over and above the internal limitations of the personalities involved, however, there are areas in both the idea and practice of ministry which can magnify the way we, as people, experience and react to our situation.

Part of the trouble lies in the biblical material, and perhaps very much in the text in St Matthew: 'Be ye therefore perfect as your Father in heaven is perfect.'[5] This is an impossible mandate for human beings. It is of course laid upon all Christians, not just upon those called to be ministers. A similar idea comes out of the Old Testament in respect of the Jewish people. It is not so much a single unequivocal text, but a general sense from several passages dealing with the righteousness of God and the chosenness of Israel in reflecting and responding to that righteousness.[6]

Failure to achieve perfection in the Old Testament brought about its own consequences — often another invasion or a social or political disaster — and was followed pretty soon by punishment, or at least this was how the events were written up for posterity. For Christians the difficulty is more insidious. In the teaching of Jesus, and indeed of the whole New Testament, the connection is less direct and explicit. Take, for example, the man who refused to sell all his goods and give to the poor;[7] the implication is not so much that he would be punished, but that he would miss out on a level of well-being and sanctity that he might otherwise have had. This is actually more difficult to handle than punishment because of its indirectness and uncertainty.

As with the biblical tradition so also with the technical vows of religion taken by monks and nuns. They were originally known as the evangelical counsels of *perfection*; even the Vatican II document on the religious life was still called *Perfectae Caritatis*.[8] The idea of perfection dies hard here despite the energetic protests of Religious over the years that their life is no more perfect than that of any other Christian.

'Perfection' has become a difficulty, despite all we could say about it being a continuous process, or about Jesus's compassion towards sinners, or St Paul's moderate definition of sin as something we all do which makes us fall short of the glory of God.[9] For constantly falling short of an ideal that is set before us is an uncomfortable emotional state. Many people who come for help to counselling centres or psychiatric clinics do so because of a subjective sense of pain and burden from their perception of a gap between themselves as they feel they are, and themselves as they feel they ought to be. In these settings the problem about perfection and perfectionism is made overt and often presented directly. Yet in the religious tradition it often goes unmarked *because* it is a built-in factor. It means that we can live all the time trying to bridge a gap, even though this is known to be a relentlessly stressful thing to try to do.

Of course, as I have indicated, this 'burden' is laid upon all followers of the Christian and Jewish traditions, and not just upon ministers or Religious. But on ministers and Religious there falls an additional load: in addition to the pursuit of goodness and holiness for themselves they have the task of encouraging others and being a model for them in their endeavours. We can see this dilemma and burden again and again in our case histories. John is horrified at himself for finding that, as a priest, he is not always caring and industrious. Anne is very burdened when she discovers how angry and resentful she can be: it does not square up to the precepts of the Religious life. Peter worries lest his marriage shows signs of failure, and his credibility as a minister and teacher gets undermined and eroded. Elizabeth is shocked by her jealousy and envy, which are unworthy and unchristian. For Robert, it is as usual rather different, as it seems that other people are trying to make him aware of a gap between potential and achievement that he himself does not feel, at least at a conscious level. Even he, though, is dedicated to perfecting the values of resignation and suppression of worldly desires.

Unconsciously, the particular form of distress in these five people reflects their earlier and childhood experiences, but the original human pattern for each of them is now *consciously* overlaid by the voice of their religious faith which both rebukes them and spurs them on to try to make good the gap between their ideal and their practice.

You may well interject at this point and say: 'Why not; is this not precisely the function and role of Christianity and other religions, to draw us on and reinforce our faltering values?' I could reply: 'But these people are in distress; some of them are developing very unpleasant physical and emotional symptoms.' The *coup de grâce* comes if you then respond: 'What can you expect if you follow Christ — are these not to be accepted as necessary and valuable sufferings?'

Here I am on difficult ground. I do not need to stay with Christianity to find examples of suffering nobly born.

I may perhaps be allowed to quote from Viktor Frankl's *Man's Search for Meaning,* his account of survival in Auschwitz, and to me one of the most moving and powerful accounts of suffering that has been accepted and worked through. Frankl himself quotes Nietszche: 'He who has a *why* to live can bear with almost any *how*';[10] and out of his terrible experience he is able to say this: 'When a man finds that it is his destiny to suffer he will have to accept his suffering and his task; his single and unique task . . . his unique opportunity lies in the way in which he bears his burden.'[11]

But Frankl was a great man, and few of us could bear what he went through; we have to take account of the tragedies of people who are crushed by a mandate to suffer, and who never get near that other proclamation of St John's Gospel: 'I am come that you may have life and have it in all its fullness.'[12] In many religious communities there is a more than usual incidence of physical illness and emotional distress. Yet even Teilhard de Chardin in his acceptance of deprivation and suffering in *Le Milieu Divin* says that the first reaction to diminishment has to be to fight it, not to accept it.[13]

I am on shaky ground here even to myself, for I have not worked out the full implications of what I am saying. Have I done justice to the experience of many, that what is accepted in response to love may itself prove life-giving and joyful? On the other hand have I really taken account of the defensive systems in all of us? There are some whose personal background is such as to make it very difficult to experience emotional well-being and happiness untinged by suffering — if there is no suffering there is a tendency to produce some. And to all of us, unless we try desperately to live for ourselves and our own pleasure alone — and indeed even if we manage it — there comes the need to deal with loss and limitation, perhaps from the early moment when we came to know that our mother cannot provide us for ever with an experience of unconditional bliss. The loss of paradise in our growing consciousness and the beginnings of the realization of the complexities of our being is a reality for each of us, and has to be if our emotional development is not to be stunted.

It seems to me that the way human beings respond to actual or threatened loss or diminishment lies on a spectrum whose extremes are the desire for total self-affirmation and fulfilment of all needs to that of self-negation and frustration of all needs and, indeed, condemnation of them when they arise. We each of us take our place on the spectrum where we *feel* most comfortable; in this placing of ourselves we often use our value system or our religious belief to help us. Hence if we, psychologically, need to suffer, Christianity will seem to bear us out. Our chosen position may not be the emotionally healthy resting-place for us, yet to move is painful, and again the pursuit of our religion can be one thing we can utilize to stop us moving.

I cannot easily assert the rights and wrongs of this behaviour. I cannot deny the fundamental right of each of us to choose our value system and to try to live in accordance with it. I cannot dispute that many would say I have got this last sentence wrong, that we do not *choose* our value system but respond to one that is somehow 'given' to us. My personal position is along the lines that we do 'choose', but our choice is by no means free, but governed by many factors of which we are not conscious. And I cannot speak to — neither would they want to hear — those who are content with their place on the spectrum or continuum, and have no doubts about the direction in which they are moving. Robert, indeed, almost comes into this category, but perhaps not quite; the fact that his bishop gets under his skin indicates that he may not be as settled as he feels he is. But with those who are questioning, who wonder if they and religion have got the balance right perhaps it is possible to speak and to take the dialogue further.

Such is the overall setting for what follows. As I write I realize that this chapter and the one which follows it really go together, almost as two sides of a coin, for this reason: this chapter is focusing on the *person* of the minister and the interaction between his or her personal history and the faith and ministry he or she has espoused. But interacting with this is the broader dimension of the relationship between ministers and their congregations. The processes which go into this relationship are the subject of the next chapter, but process and person are really inseparable.

I want, for the rest of this chapter, to take *themes* — those I feel most germane to the production of stress and strain in ministers — and to tease out particularly what may be going on below the level of our conscious awareness. I have identified nine themes; some we have already touched upon, others arise for the first time, and of course I do not claim that the list is exhaustive. I want to look at both their conscious face, and what I guess may be their unconscious depths, in the hope that what is at present denied to consciousness may come to find more conscious expression. My justification for this endeavour is simply this: the relief of strain.

It is my belief that what is unconscious exacts a toll on our energy *to the extent that we have to keep it unconscious.* Brought into consciousness it may, at one and the same time, *feel* more painful, but allow us to fire on more cylinders, free some energy previously unavailable, and enable us to make better choices, judgements and decisions.

(1) Goodness and perfection

Some ministers and lay people feel a very strong need to be 'good': good people, good Jews, good Christians — and indeed even 'perfect' examples of these. It is precisely here that the interplay between personal history and corporate faith is likely to be strong. I once saw somebody who remembered being sent off to train for the ministry with the words 'you have to be a Saint'. This followed a childhood and an experience of human parenting in which goodness and achievement were all-important, and mischief, naughtiness and 'badness' brought sorrowful reproach or heavy punishment. The human experience interacted with the received tradition of sanctity to present a truly formidable picture of the demands of priesthood. Something of the same is present in Anne's story. She understood that she had to follow the 'counsels of perfection' even more perfectly in order to justify the sacrifice her family would be making in losing her energy and contribution. We also saw how in Elizabeth's story there might be a more implicit and less conscious pressure from the memory of her relationship with her father that might make her afraid of being bad. For Peter, being bad is associated with humiliation of the kind to be avoided at all costs, and even Robert associates being 'good' with not complaining about trifles to a mother who had no time for that sort of thing.

Because of all the images that present God as, in some sense, 'Father' to us we can ally this image to our personal experience of human fatherhood. What has become more conscious to us through feminist thought and theology is that it is not only our human and religious experience of 'fatherhood' that is implicated. What of our experience of mothering, likely often to be more fundamental and sometimes more extreme? In days past we might not have been alerted to how this can affect our relationship with God, but with more recognition of the 'motherhood' of God we can come, potentially, to more awareness of what we may be bringing into our relationship with God. For example we are likely to see the motherhood of God in terms of our human experience of giving and receiving care and nurture, of our desire to be contained and held *and* our fear of being smothered and overwhelmed.

The point is this: we can *project* on to God our experience of human parenthood. In addition we can project on to ministers, as in some sense standing for God, the same things, but more of this in the next chapter.[14] So we can perceive God as being punitive to the point of being sadistic, or overindulgent. Most probably a combination is perceived; God is seen as a punitive parent in some areas, notably those of sex and anger, because these are explosive areas in our human development, and indulgent in others, often those of human weakness and dependence, because this will keep us safe from threat.

In either and any case the need to be 'good' is often paramount. For if we are not good we may evoke the disappointment of our earthly parents, and so of God, experience the anguish of being cast out, either from human love or from his embrace, and so suffer the pain of ultimate isolation and nothingness, which we may choose to call hell.

(2) Dependence

In Chapter 5 [15] we identified in our five people an ambivalent attitude to dependence, and I now want to explore this further.

Dependence *can* be a very comfortable human state; it can also be very uncomfortable, but that depends on how secure we feel in it. In Chapter 5 we noted the vicissitudes of our experience of our early dependence on our mothers — from bliss to deprivation to anger to despair to recovery. Our final 'judgement' on this experience may well have been that we do not like being dependent on other humans; they are, in our scheme of things, far too unpredictable; they put us through it.

But what of God? God is presented to us as the being who invites, and can sustain total dependence. Many prayers suggest this: 'in whom we live and move and have our being',[16] or 'by whose power we are sustained'.[17] In this dependability 'he' is much more mother to us than father. In prayer, worship and indeed in other forms of relating to him/her we are invited, and it seems enabled to express our dependency needs without the pain of our experience of being a human infant with human parents. No wonder, then, that this sense of utter dependence on God is fostered by much religious observance and tradition. It provides, as we think, a safe and adequate way of satisfying our most primitive longings and hunger.

All is well unless and until the God/parent apparently fails to respond, and we undergo a crisis of faith or something akin. We can see this in John. His theological training hadn't prepared him very well for what he had to meet; he couldn't respond with human rage, but with bodily illness. The religious life was failing Anne; she couldn't respond humanly either because anger was feared, so she had to go into depression. Elizabeth experienced a great failure of God and his human representative; her response was neither illness nor depression, but panic. Robert had tried to advance what he thought was the cause of God and had apparently failed. He became neither ill, depressed or panicky, simply very withdrawn. None of our characters was able to imitate the Job of the Bible. He resisted withdrawal from God, allowed himself to experience all the rest — ill-health, depression and anger — and seemed finally to have to succumb to the wonderful and awesome nature of God, but, and this is the point, in this finding a new well-being and separateness.

The example of Job could perhaps be the pattern of our spirituality if we could let it be. Indeed the sought-for union of the mystics with Love, Christ, can only be achieved when the loss of boundaries is the expression, paradoxically, of selfhood and separateness and not a going back to early maternal dependence. But it seems to me that quite often we cannot allow ourselves to go through the process of anger, despair and then recovery in relation to God. It is just too unpleasant, especially if the original human process and experience was not really resolved for us. If this is so then one of two things tends to happen. Either we remain in a depressed, joyless state in relation to God, often protesting that this is the necessary suffering marked out for us. Or, in that despairing mood, we commit the equivalent of suicide in relation to God and faith; we lose faith and turn right away from that dimension of being.

More likely is it that minister and people alike may get stuck in an equivalent of maternal dependence, and so order their spirituality that the next stage of anger and helplessness can never arise. If this dependence is never questioned, and God does not behave too obviously like a fallible human mother, then we can stay stuck and behave very much as children in the practice of our religion. This can mean that things like changes in teaching, doctrine or church order cannot be looked at because they would disturb the state of unquestioning infant dependence. Eden seems preferable to the toil and sense of being cast out that may accompany our steps towards growing up. In this whole process there is a particular hazard for ministers which again we shall go into further in the next chapter. If dependence on God is exalted it is likely that congregations may feel dependent on their ministers as God's human representatives. But since the minister cannot be *that* dependable, the human cycle of disappointment, disillusion and anger is likely to get played out in full force on the minister, and greatly to his strain and discomfort.

What also seems true, and would indeed be expected from our exploration is that ministers can cope better with being depended on than with being dependent. It seems, moreover, that it is most difficult for them to be dependent on other ministers, and the reasons for this are not so immediately obvious. I think it may be partly that in being dependent on another of the 'same kind' we think we run the risk of giving the other too much power over us. Because they know what is involved, perhaps we fear they will also, as did mother of old, know our vulnerable points and somehow exploit them.

(3) Self-esteem

Closely allied to the theme of dependency is that of self-esteem. It has to be because, humanly speaking, it is how we negotiate the phase of our early dependence that largely determines how we grow up thinking about ourselves and our value and worth as separate individuals.

On an external level we can see this being worked out in the conditions under which ministers live and work. Religious live in avowed poverty; this may not be actual poverty, but does involve continued dependence on the order for all the necessities of life. Secular Catholic priests are paid very poorly and remain materially dependent on their diocese. Other ministers are likewise paid below the rate for comparable professionals, and remain dependent on Mother Church for housing; this cannot but have an effect on family life, as we saw in the case of Peter and Jane. Jewish rabbis and Free Church ministers lack the independence of the 'parson's freehold' and remain very accountable, not only to the mature judgement of their congregations but also to their more irrational whims and fancies.

Such external conditions require a considerable internal maturity for survival, a freedom to feel 'OK' whatever the minister's external situation. Unfortunately this cannot be guaranteed for ministers any more than for any other people. Furthermore, as we said earlier, there are factors in a vocation to ministry which may attract people whose inner self-esteem is shaky. Such people often fear being rejected, and the position of a minister and work of ministry may seem to them to insure against this, provided, that is, that they do not rock the boat too much.

If we look at our five case histories we can see that several

of them seem to be suffering from a low sense of self-esteem
and of personal worth.

Anne's self-esteem is at rock-bottom; she feels inadequate
as a teacher and bad as a Religious. Elizabeth is in little
better state for she feels guilty about her jealous outbursts
and afraid of the weakness of her panic attacks and her fears
of going mad. Peter is doing more of a cover-up job, for his
most obvious emotion is anger: anger with his son for letting
him down and anger with his wife for not understanding and
responding to him more. But underneath lurk both his
memories of childhood humiliation, and his fears of rejection
by his congregation and neighbourhood if his marriage really
gets in a mess or his son goes right off the rails. He does not
give us, overall, the picture of a secure man who is confident
in himself and his abilities. Robert, too, is not saying that he
feels worthless or inadequate; in fact he is rather *saying* the
reverse. He is OK, and has no need of all this concern and
offers of further training. But again we wonder how he really
feels about himself in comparison with his brother, and
whether he has really recovered from the knock of the 'failure'
in Birmingham. How much would it take to burst his bubble
of confidence? John has twinges of self-doubt, but at present
he is able to be respectably ill. It is not that 'he' is not OK, but
somehow that his body has let him down.

In a word, most of our people are starting to feel *too* low for
it to be contained within the framework of their religion. But
unless and until this point sets in, religious belief can act as a
sort of defence. I suggest that it does this by what I call a
'worm and no man' theology in general and doctrine of
creation in particular. We see this in the self-deprecation of
some of the psalms.[18] A minister can cover a sense of low self-
worth by this sort of theology, but because it *is* a covering it
may go only skin-deep. On another level it can be a source of
deep and persistent emotional suffering. The pain of
worthlessness threatens to erupt all the time, and is only kept
at bay by a renewed beating of the breast until inner and
outer feelings balance again.

Sometimes all goes well until the first external failure such
as John experienced, and then the whole fragile superstructure
of the person's face-to-the-world collapses. Then a truer love

of self can be rebuilt, with help, from the inside and the end result is much more solid than the original persona or mask. But whilst the mask holds, and is a mask, it is going to be difficult for a minister to have true care, compassion and respect for those to whom he or she ministers. For we cannot really feel towards others what we do not feel for ourselves. If inwardly we despise ourselves, then at root we shall despise them. So in order to be seen to be living up to the expectations of our role we tend to live a lie and this can be a dreadful strain.

(4) Guilt

We saw in Chapter 5 on the strain of *caring*[19] the part guilt can play in the way in which we handle our caring, angry and reparative feelings. We saw, too, how in the religious dimension it has come to represent something from which we need to be delivered, and this usually happens by our attaching our guilt to a sin or Sin and then asking for forgiveness. We saw how too quick a turning of guilt into sin and forgiveness, far from taking the sense of guilt really away in the depth of our being, can in fact drive both it and the usually hostile impulses that give rise to it underground. This is what may have happened to John. We know from the earlier part of his story that he was feeling both uncaring and guilty, but what he actually ended up suffering from was physical illness rather than emotional distress, this perhaps being the only way out for him of the vicious cycle that was persecuting him.

This brings in a point we did not really explore in that chapter: the connection between guilt and placation, well reflected in the Old Testament in the notion of sacrifice. Despite assurances that the true meaning of sacrifice in the Bible is not *propitiation of an angry God* but an offering of life or at the most a free expression of sorrow for sin, the idea of propitiation somehow persists, and with it the idea that it is never achieved. The pagan sense of the greedy god who is never satisfied, and needs more sacrifice, is overtly repudiated but . . .

It seems to make no difference here that Christianity has replaced the repeated sacrifices of the Old Testament by the one sacrifice of Christ on the cross. At least I say it makes no difference, but it is, in fact, meant to make a difference. Ancient atonement theology was trying to dethrone guilt and the need for constant placation by means of this 'once and for all'. The doctrine of justification by faith seems to be saying that 'we can be as we are', and are delivered from a primitive, lasting and consuming guilt that makes us continue to mull over our sins and shortcomings. Unfortunately this is easier said than done, and though the contemplation of Christ on the cross is intended to arouse love rather than guilt this is not always what happens.

Conversion often comes about through a conviction of sin and guilt and on one level seems only to be sustained whilst our guilt is sustained even if we, so to speak, keep ourselves apart from it by the proclamation of our 'savedness'. Justification by faith can easily degenerate into the practice of justification by works, even if the 'works' are the self-conscious repeated acts of faith and trust.

In one sense we may say this is fine; religious faith allows us to feel guilty *and* encourages and spurs us on in the work of reparation or the making good for things we really have done that we regret. This corresponds, on the psychological level, to that point of growth where we begin to recognize ourselves and others as whole persons, who need to accept within ourselves and take responsibility for our 'good' and our 'bad', as distinct from an earlier stage where perhaps we could not handle them together and had to *split* them up.[20] But on another level all is not fine, and we seem to see this in both John and Anne, and to some extent in Elizabeth. As we read their stories it seems to me not too fanciful to see them as almost *persecuted* by their guilt: John by his physical illness, Anne by her depression and Elizabeth by her panic attacks. The point is that nothing is being resolved; the 'god' is relentlessly greedy for more.

We have to ask on the human level, 'Who or what is this god?', and what is the crime for which he is exacting payment? It seems to me that the god is our own guilt that persecutes us. The crime, I think, is that of being fundamentally human, having feelings — some of which are difficult for us to handle since we sense they could be destructive — but perhaps above all for *wanting*. Wanting care, nourishment, containment;

perhaps wanting them so much that we fear that our own greediness will overwhelm and empty us and the other person. These fundamental wants belong to the earliest phases of our lives and so were most strong, inevitably, in our relationships with our mothers. Some guilt at our continued desires in the face of their inevitable frustration is common to all of us, and we cannot avoid it. But if that relationship with mother was not good, and we suffered deprivation, or worse, felt that somehow we had to fulfil her wants, keep her going, care for her or even 'make her better', the resulting emotional pain of our needs can feel very great.

We can see something of this possibility in the backgrounds of John and Anne. We know John's mother was also ill and anxious, and rather unsupported by her absent husband. We know Anne had to look after her brothers and sisters. We may legitimately ask what happened to John and Anne's own wanting, and wonder if in fact they grew up deprived. Perhaps, even, this is why John lives alone: he cannot bear to want another human being.

The difficulty is that the vocation and practice of ministry seem to ask us to *give* not to *want* — certainly in relation to those we serve, and perhaps even in relation to God, with the emphasis on dedication, and sacrifice. This may not take enough account of the truth that we cannot give beyond a certain point, or that we may not have developed a self to deny or give away. Understanding this, accepting our needs, and trying to get them met rather than feel guilty about them, may be a paramount necessity for the relief of strain. Yet, because the origins of guilt are early and obscure, it is a deep and difficult thing to understand.

(5) Rivalries, jealousy and envy

We have already seen[21] that these are strong and potentially destructive feelings; furthermore there is plenty of biblical precedent for their disastrous consequences in the oft-repeated theme of the sets of two brothers. Look at Cain and Abel, Esau and Jacob, the prodigal son and the elder brother, and even, if we can let ourselves link them, at Jesus and Judas. It is not surprising, therefore, that we would like to put such emotions away from us, so ministers and congregations are often found fiercely exhorting each other to do just this. But the danger is that they will not do our bidding and go away, but will go underground instead.

Present-day Christian and Jewish communities are often riven with petty quarrels which at root seem to have to do with jealousies and envies that have got *denied* and *repressed.* The gossip in religious circles sometimes has to be heard to be believed. The unconscious envy often shows itself under the guise of 'I want to talk to you about so-and-so; I'm very concerned about them'. Under the guise of conscious caring characters can be slaughtered, in a way which is more than commensurate with the ways of the world.

Ministers and Religious are not exempt from this tendency. In our case histories Peter did not know whether his congregation or others would be compassionate to him, presumably because he had not dealt with destructive envy in himself. We see hints of more obvious jealousy and envy in Peter's wife, Jane. She minds about Peter's relationship with his work, and she seems to be jealous of his pastoral relationship with the widow in his parish. This is a familiar problem for clergy families and wives, but the great danger is of destructive jealousy creeping in and damaging the security of the marriage relationship. Elizabeth and her colleague have got locked into an envious situation, and Anne's feelings towards the younger sister in her community are a source of considerable distress to her. Robert is more complicated. He will not say he is envious of his brother, or even of his bishop for having got on in the world, but those of us who have 'nastier' minds cannot but wonder what sort of feelings he is having to keep locked away beneath his withdrawn exterior.

Envy and jealousy are humanly inescapable since we have all, from our earliest days, been put in unequal, 'unfair' situations. Yet they seem not to fit the precepts of religion, so the religious bodies have tried various ways of eradicating them. One such way has been to castigate them as sinful feelings and subdue them by discipline or spirituality. But people can suffer great strain and distress through keeping their feelings under, as we have already seen in Anne and Elizabeth.

Another, more subtle, strategy is to keep them in place by apparently making impossible the sorts of situations in which they could arise, through the operation of a hierarchy. If this is set up and everybody knows their place, as in an episcopal church or more intensely still in a religious community, feelings of jealousy can go unrecognized for longer than they can in a more democratic society where inequalities have to be seen for what they are at an earlier stage. But where there can be no jealousies it is also difficult for there to be a healthy spirit of competition and achievement, which are also important to our development. Ambition becomes a sin and potential can be snuffed out.

To try to get rid of a whole spectrum of feelings is a drastic measure; but the consequences of feeling and acting on jealousy and envy are very unpleasant. So we suppress the feelings in order to avoid the consequences, but we cannot then explore our ability to have the feelings and not allow them to go into action.

(6) Power

Power is a word not much used when talking of religious congregations or their ministers — at least not in its naked form. The nearest we get to it tends to be 'so-and-so preached a powerful sermon today'; here there is somehow the idea that it is the *words* of the sermon that were powerful and a bit detached from the voice and person who uttered them.

The other approximation to 'powerful' is the word 'charismatic', often used of a compelling person or message, but this word actually has other roots. It means 'grace', but it comes from the Hebrew for 'loving-kindness', usually applied to God himself (or herself). The root is loving-kindness, and yet the sense of power and, sometimes, autocracy — as well as of authority — emanating from charismatic figures is sometimes overwhelming, and can be greatly misused. We have only to look at the extreme fundamentalist sects to see the extent of the potential misuse through the gaining of control over the lives, minds and feelings of other human beings. Humanly speaking, power is clearly a double-edged weapon, which is maybe why we fight shy of it, at least overtly.

Where we do hear power mentioned as itself is when it is ascribed to *God*; every time we say the Lord's Prayer we proclaim 'Thine is the kingdom, the power and the glory'. The omnipotence of God is taken for granted, often extolled and sometimes feared; the power of *men* is often ascribed to others and given a perjorative overlay.

This can be disastrous for it can allow us not to recognize power in ourselves in either its positive or negative aspects. We can *project* all power on to God, and hide our own resulting sense of powerlessness under the office of minister or even literally under the vestments of that office. In this we can lose a genuine potency of person and indeed sometimes of sexuality. A male minister sometimes finds it difficult to feel a man as well as a minister, whilst a female minister can get caught in confusion as to whether struggles for recognition and equality are the same as getting caught in a power struggle. We can speculate that something of this confusion about power is present in the lives of both Elizabeth in her struggles over women's ministry, and in Robert in his studied refusal to compete.

Alternatively, we can *introject,* or swallow in, the omnipotence of God and use it as if it were our own, without really having to take individual and human responsibility for it. In extreme negative form this is when our use of power becomes nothing less than sadistic. In fact, if we give away all our power we are also vulnerable to becoming sadistic for, humanly speaking, sadism is born of humiliation and the sense of having nothing and being dominated. We see this interplay in Peter. To an outsider, Peter is very uncompassionate towards the lapses of his son, and apparently cannot reach him. He has to admit, in secret, his contempt for him, but we were told that he is not making the connection between his son and a similar occasion of humiliation in his own childhood. He is actually beginning to feel sadistic towards his son, perhaps because the situation triggers, unconsciously, those forgotten and feared feelings of humiliation.

This is an all too common human scenario, but can become more complicated by the religious dimension. In general terms the problem lies in the *mix* of the 'divine' and the 'human' which we are likely to make. We can consciously lose all our power before God, but at the same time unconsciously take it back and use it sadistically against others.

It may seem like heresy to talk of sadism in the Christian context. Surely it is out of place in a religion that extols love and compassion? Yet this is one of the areas where religion can reinforce, in an unhelpful way, our human tendency to denial of things unpleasant. Most of us find it very difficult to get in touch with our sadistic side: it seems very nasty and taboo. In religious systems the whole area of power, domination *and* sadism can easily get tamed, legalized or otherwise driven underground. There it can flourish rapaciously and destructively.

We may not want to recognize ourselves here, for it is a most unpleasant subject. Christians sometimes think of the Jewish tradition as being stuck in the 'eye for an eye' stage, but in fact it may be that the Jewish tradition deals with this area more openly, and, in the end, more healthily. Christianity talks of love, but perhaps we should rather talk of compassion, for that word implies that we have probably begun to recognize, accept and work on our *un*compassionate side. If we slide away into the word 'pity' we are off key again, for pity allows us to 'look down' from a powerful detached high place. Compassion requires empathy and so brings the whole area nearer home.

The particular strain for ministers comes just because the area is difficult and often *repressed,* yet by their inevitable leadership role, ministers are vulnerable to it. The extent to which we have not faced it will both cause *us* strain and expose us to the risk of 'acting out' our 'nasty' side on *others* without necessarily realizing that this is what we are doing.

Another problem for ministers and their congregations, which is intimately connected with a lot of the foregoing, is that humanly speaking we are no doubt frightened as to where the extremes of our nastiness could lead us. This may be why we expend energy in putting them away from us. I am advocating that if we can look at them and allow them into consciousness then they may in fact become easier to bear and handle. But that is in a sense walking at first by faith. We each of us have to try this approach and see if it is so.

We have also seen, in the discussion of the theme of power, how our ideas about our make up and what goes on in us, have an interrelation to our ideas about God. If we begin to accept the dark side of ourselves does this also mean that we shall suspect and have to face the possibility of a darker side to God? And if so where would that leave us? Would we be at the mercy of an ambivalent, capricious or even malignant force? This was the question of Job, and I am not sure that he necessarily received a comforting answer.[22]

There are immense philosophical and theological problems here, connected with the problem of evil, and I do not propose to go into them now. I am wanting rather to say that they have emotional reverberations that may strain us considerably, and disturb us at levels below that of the intellectual discussion of truth. I am suggesting that the way we reduce strain on ourselves as ministers is to undo some of the *splits* we are likely to have between our 'good' and our 'bad' sides. What we may also have to face in so doing are changes in our idea of God, *along the same lines.* We have to explore the possibility that in God we hope for the *integration* of 'good' and 'bad', not the *absence* of the bad. This idea may actually feel very disturbing to us because we have linked our ideas of God to the meaning of *all* existence, not just *my* or *our* existence. If he is not integrated will the creation survive?

This reflection may seem like a nightmare, and the more mature parts of our faith may be able to cope with these sorts of questions, but we may find that primitive thoughts of God rise up from the shadowy recesses of our less mature being when we are most unprepared for them. At least when he is being primitively all-good, that may not hurt us too much, but primitively bad or primitively mixed — these can feel very frightening.

I think this section is important, because it is a hard area faced by ministers and lay people alike. The strain on ministers, though, may be the greater. Once again they stand in the representative position, and as the recipients of all sorts of projections, both about themselves and about God, the purpose of the latter being to keep at bay frightening alternatives. Being at the receiving end of a constant and powerful projection is never easy.

Perhaps I could again end this section with a piece of more personal reflection. It was in this area that I most came a cropper when I was active in ministry. I was exploring, or so I thought, the themes of good and bad, in God as well as human beings. What I did not realize was that I was exploring them primarily intellectually; such was the limit of my awareness at the time. I had not really internalized what I was saying and was out of touch with my deeper feelings. So I did not realize how potentially disturbing some of what I was saying was — to others, certainly, but also to myself. So I strained myself, was hurt by the reaction my efforts provoked, and probably strained others.

This drew my attention to another point. By reason of the emphasis of our training (and sometimes also of our personality) our head may be ahead of or out of touch with our heart. This I think was probably some of John's trouble; whether he was right to locate its source in his theological training rather than in himself is not so clear. Be that as it may, in more general terms our theological sophistication is not necessarily matched by our level of emotional maturity. Some of our congregations may have got it more right than we have, some may have got it less right. For a young minister, particularly, this is a difficult area, but it affects all of us.

(7) Authority and parent-child models

We have already touched, in the sections on dependency and power, on how difficult an area this can be. But there is a little more that needs to be said here and more still to be taken up in the next chapter.[23]

In some traditions the minister is known as 'Father', and all the connotations of that word get attached to him. For ministers themselves the problem is taken to the next layer up, for bishops are known as fathers-in-God. There is not the same *overt* titling of women ministers, and from the earlier section on the power of woman/mother[24] we can see that we might have very good reasons for not wanting to think of them as 'Mother'. It does, of course, happen in women's religious communities, but this often both expresses and facilitates a regression to a family model of functioning that is unhelpful to a group of people trying to live together as adults.

The parental model is thus operative in the religious bodies, and is not confined only to persons; Scripture and tradition can also take on a quasi-parental role, and there tends to be both acceptance of and ambivalence towards it. The source of this acceptance and ambivalence is not too hard to tease out given all our earlier reflections on the effect on us of our early family life. We both want it and parents, and don't want it and parents. What often then happens is that we get away from parents and get caught in an 'adolescent' rebellion against all authority. This tendency can again be found throughout the religious bodies, in ministers *and* congregations. Congregations often want to cut the minister down to size; ministers come to resent any incursion of the bishop/boss on their autonomy.

It is not easy, given this climate, to find a right and helpful expression of either leadership or authority. Bishops are called to exercise strong leadership, resolve disputes, etc.; ministers get vested with authority rather similar to the authority of God. When ministers or bishops fail in something they cannot live up to the disappointment and disillusionment can be intense, just as it is with parents, and hard to bear for the people concerned. The problem Yo-Yos and is endemic perhaps to the ordering of all human societies, but it can be made more difficult in the religious world because of the overshadowing image of the authority of God. What can get lost is a sense of *personal and individual* responsibility.

(8) Sexuality

Sexuality is one of our most powerful personal drives, capable of giving us great joy and great suffering, and it is therefore not surprising that it causes difficulty to many people. Religious faith and practice have sought to help channel this strong desire by, in effect, hedging it around with various prohibitions and prescriptions, based on the will of God as discerned through the Bible and tradition. But just because it is possible to 'lean' on the given tradition and not really to come to terms in ourselves with our sexuality, religious people have more difficulties in this area than might have been expected. For the priest or minister problems can arise on several levels.

First, we are not necessarily 'expert' in dealing with problems in this field, but they are often presented to us.

Furthermore we are often made the possessor of intimate secrets under difficult circumstances; whereas counsellors take care not to muddle counselling and friendship, to set aside specific and limited time for counselling and not to meet clients outside this, as ministers we of necessity meet our congregations in many different 'work' settings and often socially as well. We may also have become accustomed to people dropping in on us at all hours, and to some extent us on them. This pattern alone can make for difficulties. We saw in Peter's story that he was constantly visiting a bereaved parishioner to the point where Jane was getting angry and suspicious. Her suspicions may have been born of jealousy alone with nothing behind them, or it may be that Peter is vulnerable to visiting female parishioners in need of comfort after loss. John was not enjoying the over-assiduous attentions of his female parishioners, and at this stage we are not sure why.

These boundary problems are hard enough, but if we are also uncomfortable, consciously or unconsciously, with our own sexuality then the difficulties are compounded. For, all unknowingly, we can use the tradition as a sort of defence. It is possible to invoke it too quickly, not really want to hear what is said, and adopt an almost punishing attitude by a heavy use of the 'law'. Alternatively we can get caught in a compulsive, almost voyeuristic, desire to hear more and more when this is not really appropriate.

It takes considerable self-awareness to be able, without excessive strain, both to keep and use the values of the religious tradition, and to empathize with what is being presented. The issue comes up in many ways; what are we to say to the homosexual person who comes caught in a conflict between his or her feelings and desires and the received tradition of the Church, or those wanting to divorce and remarry, or those bothered about excessive sexual feelings or a lack of any at all. We do not easily know what people want or need from us; do they want permission, absolution, help in standing by their values, help in putting back their emotional defences? Our dilemma in responding will contain our feelings about our own sexuality, the tradition of the Church and the unconscious interplay between the two.

These are the sorts of things that may stress us on the level of the work we *do,* but there is another whole level of potential stress that may assail us on the level of the person we *are.* This is most difficult for ministers whose orientation or lifestyle does not conform either to the norms of the tradition or those of the milieu in which they are set. For example, it is difficult for a rabbi not to be married, whilst in Christianity the celibate tradition is accepted, respected and valued, and indeed laid on priests of the Roman tradition. This last can cause persistent and sharp suffering to people if their awareness of their sexuality comes only after their ordination to the priesthood or entrance into the religious life. We have already wondered about Anne's personal history in this respect, and what it must have been like for her being pitchforked from a convent school into the mixed staffroom of a comprehensive.

For ministers of all traditions a homosexual orientation is likely to be a source of suffering since the expression, if not the fact of it, is at variance with the official teachings of nearly all the religious bodies. The danger for some here is that the tendency can stay latent and unconscious — perhaps it dare not be admitted to consciousness — and so energy and creativity are sapped. For others, the orientation can be admitted, but no expression allowed: this imposes suffering and loneliness of a different kind, often excruciatingly coupled with an intense resentment that celibacy is being demanded, not chosen. We wonder why John lives alone; we are not told what his orientation is, nor indeed much of his private life. Should he be homosexual and struggling with it, then this could well be contributing to his stress, and also probably increasing his loneliness. For yet others a homosexual orientation can be lived out almost defiantly, sometimes in fear of discovery, sometimes with a tendency to promiscuity — this latter the more sad and dangerous with the AIDS threat. Even if a stable relationship is made then this is often pushed into a landlord/lodger pattern, which is hardly satisfactory for the self-esteem of the couple concerned.

This is a point where being a minister impinges very much on private life in a way that can cause intense suffering. There are others; if a minister is single the congregation may be consciously or unconsciously both wanting to marry him or her off, and yet at the same time not wanting him or her to have an exclusive relationship. Either way this feels very intrusive to the minister. For the married minister the problems are different. We have touched on them with Peter and Jane, and will go into this more in the next chapter.[25] Suffice it to say here that the current discipline in the churches on ministers whose marriages have broken down, or ordinands coming from divorced backgrounds is tough, though some would say not more so than for any other church member. It *is* different, though, because the whole of life and livelihood is bound up in ministry — hence Peter's anxiety.

For all of us, whatever our personal lifestyle or state, if we are avoiding some aspects of our sexuality and are not aware of this we are likely both to *project* them, and to be at the receiving end of other people's projections of their sexuality if they also are unable to look at what they are doing. We or a parishioner may think the other is the seducer when in fact the feelings and desires belong nearer home. We shall look more at this process of projection in the next chapter;[26] suffice it here to assert that sexuality is a ripe ground for projection just because it is so powerful and aspects of it tend easily to get split off and denied to consciousness.

(9) Loneliness

In a strange way this theme follows on from that of sexuality, for this reason: as adult human beings one of the ways in which we bridge gaps between each other and assuage our loneliness is through sexual intimacy. So for those ministers for whom this is not an actual or potential possibility, the problem of loneliness is intensified.

In practical terms, a congregation may itself be more demanding if they know there is no spouse or family to make legitimate demands on their pastor, or even to shield him from them. So anyone in a single position has to be more rather than less disciplined in safeguarding times when he or she is not available. This can mean coping with others' resentment that the minister has apparently no ties and no cares, within the ever-strong assumptions of the *stereotype* of perpetual and total availability. In any case, not to be available is not always easy if we do not, for example, have a clear idea of what we *want* to be doing on our days off. It may feel better to work than to do nothing and see nobody.

Some people make friends easily, some do not; those who do not may have chosen the way of pastoral ministry precisely to hide this lack. But even when possessed of a network of friends all the problems of confidentiality come up: how much can you say about your job and pastoral situations that are worrying you to your friends, particularly if they are from the same area? This dilemma is not confined to the single or the religious, but is also present to the married and can be a source of conflict in that relationship to which we shall return later.

Belonging to a religious order does not automatically assuage the sense of loneliness either, as Anne found; in fact the dictum 'we can be more lonely with other people than anywhere else' can be horribly true in this instance.

In summary, the work of ministry is inherently lonely; people who become ministers may have personal difficulties in this area and the two interact with each other.

These nine themes cover some of the stresses inherent in *being* a minister. So far we have looked at where they are rooted in our personalities and personal histories; we need to turn now to the *processes* that go on between us and others which can both exacerbate existing strain and create more.

Notes

1. Especially chs. 1, 2, 5.
2. See pp. 137ff.
3. See ch. 2, pp. 45, 46.
4. See ch. 10, pp. 192—4, 203—5.
5. Matthew 5.48.
6. See, for example, Jeremiah 33.14—16; Isaiah 42, 1—4; but throughout the OT the whole idea of covenant, from that made with Abraham (Genesis 17) onwards.
7. Mark 10.17—22.
8. W. M. Abbott, ed. *The Documents of Vatican* II, Geoffrey Chapman 1965, 'Decree on the Renewal of the Religious Life', pp. 462—81.
9. Romans 3.23.

10. Cited in V. Frankl *Man's Search for Meaning,* Hodder and Stoughton 1964, new ed. 1987, p. 76.
11. ibid., p. 78.
12. John 10.10.
13. Teilhard de Chardin, *Le Milieu Divin*, Fontana 1957, Part II, ch. 3, esp. pp. 83, 84.
14. See ch. 9, pp. 181−7.
15. See p. 102.
16. R. M. Benson (1825−1915) in A. S. T. Fisher *An Anthology of Prayers,* Longmans 1964, no. 46.
17. Samuel Johnson (1709−1784) in *An Anthology of Prayers,* op. cit. no. 91.
18. e.g. Psalm 22, v. 6ff.; Psalm 38.3−8.
19. See pp. 99, 101-2.
20. See ch. 6, n. 24.
21. See ch. 2, pp. 42−3.
22. See C. G. Jung *Answer to Job*, Routledge and Kegan Paul 1954.
23. See ch. 9, pp. 184−6.
24. See ch. 7, pp. 134−6.
25. See ch. 9, pp. 187−91.
26. See ch. 9, p. 184.

NINE

Transferring Feelings —
Myth and Ritual

I have entitled this chapter 'Transferring Feelings — Myth and Ritual', and all four words require some explanation and amplification.

I am not going to take them in the right order and will start with 'feelings'. For it is, above all, our feelings, rather than our beliefs or thoughts, which contribute most to our subjective sense of strain as ministers. Furthermore, what goes on in us unconsciously can be stronger than any conscious feelings, and potentially more difficult and even destructive just because, to the extent that it remains unconscious, it is out of our own mediating and moderating control.

Even the feelings we are aware of may be very powerful and erupt in what — to others, certainly, and sometimes, provided we have some insight, to ourselves — seem to be the wrong places, at the wrong times and with excessive intensity. Take, for example, Elizabeth, who found herself having uncharacteristically angry and jealous feelings towards her colleague, and a sense of disappointment and disillusion with her vicar — who, after all, is not there to sort her out, he is her boss. Or John, who began to feel worried and angry about the over-attachment of certain of his parishioners without really knowing why. Or Anne, whose sudden consciousness of angry feelings in a religious life previously unhealthily free of them led to an increased sense of depression and doubt about the whole heart of her vocation as a nun.

Robert is a little different here and exemplifies an intensification of the transferral problem. All he could allow himself to feel was a mild irritation at the well-meaning but blundering efforts of his superiors to interest him in activities he did not want to be interested in. *We,* reading his story from outside, guess at feelings of doubt and low self-worth, but he himself seems to be keeping them well out of consciousness; he really does not know that this is what is going on inside him.

Robert is thus the prototype of the *unaware* person who is spared the pain of strong disturbing feelings; the others are certainly more aware of having feelings. They are also aware in varying degrees that some of the intensity and some of the direction of their feelings do not really fit their actual situation, but they are trapped in them and cannot sort them out. So John gets ill, Elizabeth gets panicky, Anne and Peter and Jane stay more in touch with what they are feeling but cannot resolve anything. It's a powerful and sorry state of affairs for them all.

In a wider context than these people, what if, as ministers, we feel unaccountably (to us) angry at some reform to the liturgy or church order, or, equally unaccountably, judgemental when asked to minister to an Aids sufferer. In the case of the latter to discover that we *feel* judgemental when by all usual standards compassion is called for is an extremely disturbing experience. To find in ourselves a subjective sense of hate towards the apparently insatiable demands of parishioners where previously there had been a sense of care and commitment is equally very disturbing. Our feelings may persist and even intensify despite all our internal efforts to sort them out, and despite the fact that we manage not to act upon them. For we are not told that John was actually anything but polite and caring to his parishioners if they caught him when he was in the mood to dodge them, but the feeling wouldn't go away. Anne made heroic efforts for a long time not to let her feelings show.

If we find ourselves experiencing something of all this we need to ask ourselves, since often we dare not ask anyone else as we feel too ashamed: 'What on earth is going on, in me, and all these other people and even the Church or the world, that it all feels upside-down and even a bit mad at times?'

One of the things that is likely to be happening when we have persistent inappropriate feelings that will not go away is that these very feelings may not really 'belong' to this present situation but are *displaced* or *transferred* from another current or earlier situation involving different people. For example we can find ourselves wanting to kick the cat, the dustmen or anybody else around without apparently any real cause, *until* we can allow ourselves to remember that actually we were very fed up with the churchwarden when he or she called a few hours earlier with yet another useless query about our carefully worked out agenda for the AGM. We couldn't allow ourselves to feel fed up with them at the time; after all we need them and are even in some sense accountable to them; not many people want that job, and we might get somebody far worse. We have to work with them.

If and when we stop kicking the cat and instead twig about our real feelings towards our encounter with the churchwarden it is possible that we might remember something else about that encounter. At one point it suddenly felt like being back at home as a child, when one or other of our parents kept barging in on our model railway project or doll's house, with senseless questions as to what we were up to, and equally senseless, to us, advice as to how to do it better! 'How much of the room is it going to take up? Would you please be careful of the carpet; if you did it this way you'd have it finished in time for tea . . .' However that memory came into our minds for a minute and went out just as quickly as one of those flashes from the past — quite irrelevant, we say, to what's going on now. In any case, we reiterate to ourselves, we are now the boss, not the churchwarden, and we are both the same age. Our slight feelings of irritation, and even more, our slight feelings of inferiority are in this situation quite inexplicable and quite inexcusable; or so we tell ourselves and return to working off our feelings on the equivalent of the cat!

A lot of the time we do not even notice what we are doing. We discharge our feelings on 'the cat' fairly mindlessly unless our choice of 'cat' objects strongly. If that happens or if we have feelings that we sense are *particularly* inappropriate to our state in life, like a minister who feels extremely angry during the Eucharist or becomes aware of strong sexual feelings when counselling people in the intimacy of his or her study, we begin to take notice and/or to become disturbed by them. But until and unless this happens we are often living by and in a myth.

I am here using the word 'myth', the third word of the title of this chapter, in a manner which I think is rather near its biblical roots. The myths of the Old Testament were stories which were not meant to be taken as literally true, but which, on another level, expressed deep truths about the individuals concerned or about life — truths that could not easily be apprehended on the logical rational level. For example, the Fall story in Genesis 3 is not to be taken as a literal *explanation* of how suffering, labour and sin came into being, but much more as a *description* at a deep level of the price of consciousness and the awareness of separation and desire.

As with Genesis, so too with the story of our manifest human feelings. They should not always be taken at face value, but as an indicator of another story that is going on inside us: possibly a more fundamental story of our life and relationships as they have developed over time and situations. For Anne the 'top' story was that of a disturbed relationship in the present with one of the sisters in the community; the bottom story was the replay of her formative childhood years in relationship with her real sister.

As in biblical myth, both our 'stories' or levels are real, but it is the underneath story that is exerting the power, even stranglehold, and it needs to be recognized and understood. There are often unresolved elements in it that are insidiously but persistently demanding our attention, snarling up our present lives and diminishing our inner freedom.

It is often our feelings, rather than anything else, that give us the first clue as to the presence and nature of this underlying story. If we take no notice of them then they may have to speak more loudly, first by an increase in their intensity and, if this fails, sometimes by action or, if this seems disallowed by our conscience, through our illnesses or even our breakdowns. We see something of this mechanism in the stories of John, Anne, Peter and Elizabeth; the initial twinges of feeling do not seem to have been heard, and more drastic reaction threatens.

But the unravelling of our feelings and the action associated with them is not easy. The processes that have gone into making them what they are are often very complicated, and involve more than just ourselves. Furthermore, they are often designed to hide the truth from us, for the 'truth' might seem overwhelmingly disturbing. We have already indicated in earlier chapters[1] how this might be especially so in the area of religion and ministry because we are dealing with some of the most raw and fundamental areas of human life.

Before we go on to relate this to the themes of the last chapter, I would like to take a little while to look at one form of possible defence against feeling that we have not yet really mentioned. Its use is not only and always negatively defensive; it can also act as a container and transmitter of feeling, but in overuse it becomes unhelpfully constricting. It is found in many aspects of human life, but I think the particular nature of religion and religious observance, as this has developed, means that it will certainly get used and sometimes overused or abused in this context. I am referring to 'ritual', the fourth word of this chapter's heading.

The use of ritual

Ritual and rituals are not something that are peculiar to religious bodies: they exist in all walks of life. Small children often have long and complicated rituals designed to protect them against harms they cannot easily articulate to grown-ups. One such ritual is the lining up of toys in bed every night in an exact and same order as a sort of protection against the darkness and unknownness of night, and you can probably think of countless others. When such rituals persist into adult life and become very complicated and entrenched the life of the person and of those around them tends to become over-controlled and restrictive, as in the case of severely obsessional and compulsive behaviour. But in its mild form we probably all tend to preserve some rituals; indeed we may be scarcely aware of them unless they come to be a source of irritation to whoever we live with! There are countless rituals to do with hospital life and the practice of medicine; we have seen how the need for them may be the more intense because of the primitive, often life-and-death quality of the activity. The ritual of the law-court can help to keep manageable the essentially difficult and distasteful nature of the exercise of sitting in judgement upon and sentencing other human beings. The most sinister use of ritual we see perhaps in the vocabulary devised for carrying out and disguising the horrors of the Holocaust, and in the ritualistic way in which the 'final solution' of extermination was in fact implemented in the death camps.

We can say that the purpose of rituals is to contain the underlying story of the myth, in such a way that its essential truth is allowed to go on living and developing. The underlying story may of course be either benign or malignant in essence. In the case of Nazi Germany it was malignant, and the ritual preserved this in all its malignancy without confronting either the actual perpetrators or those who could not but witness or hear about, even from afar, the 'ritual', for example, of the railway transports, but who dared not let themselves assess its underlying significance.

Religious ritual, and indeed liturgy, whether or not combined with outward ritual, has the task of containing the great myths and truths of religion in such a way that ideally we can go on assimilating and growing in them, without being overwhelmed by them. This is true even of the ordinary daily or weekly worship of Church and Synagogue, and we began to see some of the potential strains on the minister brought about by his essential and symbolic role in this in Chapter 7.

Ritual in one form or another is endemic to the life of a religious body; it is one form of initiating and maintaining the deep underneath story of relationship with the Almighty.

I wonder if we could stop for a moment and ask ourselves, even if this does not happen to form a large part of our actual work, what it really feels like to officiate at countless funerals or even marriages. These occasions carry great and fundamental despairs, fears or hopes. For the people centrally concerned they are often very intense once- or twice-off events in their lives, but what of the minister who has to officiate? Are we not likely to run the risk of devitalizing the occasion through overexposure to its ritual form? This is not exactly using the ritual to defend against feelings, but rather losing our feelings in the outward form of the ritual. We can also lose any expectation that it can ever be any different.

But there are other times when we may need the outward

form to help us cope with our over exposure to people's — and our own — pain. For what does it feel like to be constantly ministering in a land such as violence-torn Northern Ireland where death and hatred are never far away, or to have to preach, as did the Archbishop of Canterbury, at something like the memorial service[2] for those who died in the 1987 Zeebrugge disaster. Even the annual re-enactment of the occasion of Remembrance in Whitehall is potentially tough on those who take a central part in it. On a more everyday level what is it like to be admitted constantly to the innermost thoughts of people with whom we are involved in hospital chaplaincy or even ordinary parish or congregational pastoral care? More intimately still, what of the pressures, for those who are of this persuasion, of hearing people's darkest and most difficult secrets through the sacrament of confession?

The pressures of intimate contact are there for all of us who work with the deeper part of people in any of the caring professions. Sometimes what we are hearing really gets inside us and we can get exhausted and even overwhelmed, or worse, not quite notice that this is happening until the process in us has gone rather far. In some sort of instinctive move towards survival we then operate some defence or cut-off. It is from this total cut-off that ritual can save us; its outward form can help us contain our feelings and go on. But if we ourselves have a low toleration for strong feelings and need to defend ourselves hard against them, then this cut-off point comes too soon and completely and the ritual becomes, not the living container, but the *tomb* of feeling.

These considerations are not relevant only to the 'one-off' occasions of individual or corporate celebration and pain, but also hold for the more everyday life of the religious bodies. They apply most obviously to those traditions with a rich liturgical and sacramental dimension but are not absent from the others.

In those religious bodies that rely heavily upon the ministry of the Word, ritual is present but it is focused on the operation of the Word itself, the Word of God in the New Testament and the Torah of the Old. The reading and proclaiming of the Word often takes on a life of its own as powerful and compelling as that of a very rich liturgy. The big evangelistic rallies and long sermons in Evangelical churches often exhibit a very definite ritual, in the manner of delivery of the Word or sermon, making much use of particular modulations and resonances of the human voice. Such 'ritual' can be almost overlooked, because it does not, initially, seem like ritual. But its power should not be underestimated, both as a container of instincts and feelings, and at other times — sometimes constructively and sometimes almost destructively — as a way to break down personal defences and free feelings that it may not then be very easy to control. A minister in this situation is inevitably exposed to the whole dimension of power,[3] in a way that resonates with and is amplified by a crowd situation. It is his or her voice that is making an impact, making things happen, and his or her personality that is operative, for good or ill. To my mind the burden of this on an individual minister can be, and the responsibility has to be, tremendous.

In those traditions where worship has a more obviously ritualistic dimension, the power of the act itself and the pressures on the minister in a representative position are perhaps less nakedly obvious, but no less present and active. The purpose of liturgy and sacrament is, as I see it, to function as a *symbol,* and in this to do almost opposite things at the same time. On the one hand it is to contain what could be an almost unbearably powerful reality so that it can be assimilated and integrated by the worshippers, and secondly it is to free and enlarge the capacity of those same worshippers, including the celebrant or officiant, to explore and take in more of that reality.

Let me attempt to explain a little further what I mean. The Seder celebration of the Passover, commemorating the deliverance from the oppression of Egypt, or the eucharistic celebration of the passion and resurrection of Christ both attempt to re-present to us, at a pace we can tolerate, the re-enacting of oppression and deliverance, and the re-experiencing of an act of love, hate, murder and reconciliation. The symbols used then take on the power carried in less ritualized situations by the Word. There are also times when the symbolic dimension is even more heightened, as in the liturgy for the Jewish Day of Atonement or the Christian Holy Week liturgy. At these points we have a choice, whether to apprehend the truth, and trust that we can keep this revelation at a pace and intensity our humanness can tolerate, or to let the ritual somehow domesticate the truth, which may make it safer for us, but also runs the risk of the occasion becoming one of empty, lifeless ritual.

We can probably all recall memories both of powerful and of dead liturgy. When I lived in a religious community we were implicitly, if not explicitly, warned not to overstrain in Holy Week, because of the very powerful nature of the liturgy; conversely there have been times when I have participated in an occasion of high and prolonged ritual to come away asking myself what it was all about, as somehow nothing seemed to connect with the depths of me. Either I have shut off, or there has been a shutting off of communication in the liturgy itself, and the most common culprit here is an overemphasis on the exactitude and outward form of the ritual.

If we are in the role of minister in such liturgical services then we are in a central sensitive position *but* we could imagine that our humanness is somehow protected. After all we act according to a prescribed form, we often wear special clothes for the occasion which somehow disguise our humanness, and the measured liturgical walk always seems to me not quite human! This, though, is all on the level of the 'top level' story of the myth. There is also the powerful, underneath level exerting a strain on us, though this may operate, at least to an extent, below the level of our conscious awareness.

Consider, for example, an ordinary celebration of the Eucharist. I have to use this, rather than an occasion from Jewish or more Word-centered worship, because it is with this that I am most familiar. On the *visible* level the minister acts as president or convenor on an occasion of solemn sharing in the context of remembrance and thanksgiving for our salvation. The setting is essentially symbolic, and all Christian bodies have repudiated crude ideas of re-enactment of sacrifice. We proclaim that the presence of Christ is real in the bread and wine, at the same time saying that this is not a literal presence, though our efforts to describe this in words through the ages have not always been successful or understood. Revisions of the liturgy have heightened the corporate aspect and tried to lessen the impact of the role of the solitary celebrant.

Underneath, however, I am suggesting that there is a different story again. This story *does* have within it the elements of remembering a perfect sacrifice, of our desire to communicate on a deep level with our creator and to take something in from him/her as well as from each other. We are concerned with cleansing ourselves before we enter into this encounter. We receive him/her under the symbolic and gentle form of bread and wine, but the very language presents us with a challenge to our more primitive selves. We are virtually eating our God, as members of cannibalistic tribes ate each other for survival and sustenance. There is also a heightening of intimacy, sometimes with relative strangers, such as we would not expect in any other gathering, and an element of fusion with each other and with the Almighty. This underneath story is, humanly speaking, both primitive and explosive.

In the underneath story the celebrant is more than a presidential figure. He or she has to carry the symbols, whether we like it or not, of the Old Testament priests offering sacrifice, as the human representative of man to God, and, perhaps more frighteningly, of the representative of God to man. As the human person who presides over the feast, he or she makes possible and sets in motion the enormous symbolic act. We can see the Eucharist as a container of some of our most primitive feelings and desires; it contains them so that we can make a more articulate response from our more developed selves, and come to participate in mature acts of thanksgiving and love. And it is the function of the celebrant to hold and carry this transformation. However undefended we may be we could not easily *feel* all this consciously and stay sane, for it would be too overwhelming; but unconsciously the pressure will be there.

Here we have a direct connection with the theme of the last chapter: the pressure on ministers to *be* special people. Yet it is a pressure that we tend to be unaware of just because it is so ordinary and so usual a part of our ministry. But it is through this representative liturgical role that we shall experience, even at an inarticulate unconscious level, ourselves as we are at present in relationship to goodness, dependence, power, and guilt. So the liturgical role imposes a considerable strain as our personal being reverberates to it. Hopes and feelings are *transferred* on to us by the congregation and tune in, amplify or conflict with our own. Yet this is a source of strain of which we have taken very little account.

For less sacramental religious communities the 'underneath' role of the minister will differ less from the 'top' role. Our personality is used more directly and there is less of a fusion of the individual person with the wider unseen realities. The underneath story is most likely to be the compulsion to be the perfect imitator of the historical person of Jesus, or the perfect descendent of the great rabbis: still stressful, but without so much merging of the actual person with the greater-than-personal.

We have talked so far of the *corporate* rituals of religion and religious sacraments. But there are also the more personal sacraments when the minister is in much more direct and intimate contact with a parishioner or possibly a group of parishioners or congregants. I am referring, of course, to the sacraments of confession, anointing and laying-on of hands. The actual practice of these is not now confined to those in formal ministry, although the formal authoritative exercise of them is, and as ministers we act both symbolically and humanly here.

The strains for ministers in this sort of ministry are not the same as those that pertain to the 'larger' liturgical role. There the stress comes from being caught up in the hugeness of the theme, of almost being depersonalized within it, with the human undercurrents flowing underneath in a strangely 'cut off' manner. Here the difficulty comes from the personal nature of the encounter, and its very intimacy.

In the sacraments of forgiveness and healing a minister is still asked to be the channel of an activity of God, not one that is circumscribed by human boundaries. But he or she is a human being ministering to another human being and human qualities are needed too.

These qualities are minimized in the sacrament of confession, at least in its older form, when face-to-face contact was limited. But even then there was a strain on the priest: of listening, and being compassionate, of making the sacrament meaningful and not *just* a ritual. And of course since confession is not usually practised in isolation from the rest of religious life, except by those who deliberately choose to go somewhere special for this exercise, there is the added difficulty of meeting in other and possibly social contexts those whose innermost and most shameful secrets we have heard, or, among ministers, the person who has heard one's own. It is a situation that most counsellors and psycho-therapists would choose to avoid, and yet it is one that ministers face frequently. That they mostly negotiate it pretty well does not mean that it is not a strain, for either party. The more recent practice of hearing confessions face to face, often in the context of an informal talk, certainly makes the occasion more meaningful, but also heightens the personal dimension, the intimacy and so the strain. It is not uncommon for a priest to find that some of his most 'attached' parishioners come from among his penitents, because the situation is objectively a difficult one to contain. The liturgy and the sacrament try to do so but do not always succeed. In my opinion they sometimes do not because the exercise requires maturity on both sides, and maturity in the religious dimension is something that any person may or may not have. For religion can be the vehicle for his or her more regressed and primitive parts, and when this is so such situations can be difficult. It is then that a minister may come to feel that he or she is almost being asked to be a real rather than symbolic parent, and this is exceedingly difficult to manage within the confines of an ordinary human relationship. The 'God' dimension may be brought in to help, but this sometimes only puts to bed the problem where it sleeps rather than is resolved.

The sacraments of healing carry similar difficulties, on both 'religious' and 'human' levels. In them the minister sets out to be a channel for the healing power of God, of which the human act is a symbol.

On the religious level ministers are both tempted to omnipotence — to push back the laws of nature — and vulnerable to great anxiety about failure, or success, in this endeavour. But the human symbol is also strong, involving the human sense of touch, and it is not surprising that it can sometimes also evoke the memories of parental caresses, particularly since illness often makes us regress in our level of functioning. This does happen; it can be felt by the participants or it can be felt by the minister. As ministers we can get overwhelmed, on the human level, by our prescribed role in the sacraments. It is not impossible for our boundaries to go and the occasion feel almost too real for emotional comfort. Much of the time we are inwardly organized so as to be able to contain these aspects and experiences of our ministry. In fact, of course, we may have ourselves so well organized and defended against them that we are not sensitive to them, and are unaware that other participants may be having difficulty. If occasionally the human side breaks through on us, either in extreme and prolonged dependency or in the emergence of sexual feelings in either the minister or the recipient, this tends to be the trigger for panic stations and the sense that something has gone very wrong. In our panic we sometimes act rejectingly and hurtfully, by precipitately withdrawing our ministry instead of trying to understand, maybe talk it through, and use the experience as a way of growth. In a way it is not such a surprise that it happens, given the nature of the exercise, but rather that it does not seem to happen more often.

If this sort of experience becomes frequent for us it does give us an indication that we have got stuck somewhere and may need some help in sorting ourselves out, and it is the admission of this that can be the difficulty. For there is a tendency in us to think with shame, 'How can it ever have happened; it doesn't seem to happen to anyone else and it must be awful?'.

This perhaps is part of the myth that it doesn't happen to anyone else. Given the nature of the liturgy and sacraments it would be surprising if their rituals did not have the capacity to disturb us as well as give us a great sense of satisfaction in our ministry. They can be a powerful means by which our feelings can move, transfer themselves and intensify, as well as a container in which they can be borne and carried.

Ways of transferring feelings

The movement of feelings in the liturgy and through rituals is not all inappropriate. The role of the minister in liturgy *is* a special and representative one and, with the exceptions that began to surface in the last section on the more personal sacraments, the problem seems to be more the intensification — to an unbearable degree for the minister concerned — of feelings that are not inappropriate to the role, rather than those feelings being directed at the wrong person, *per se.*

But in the last section we began to approach the area of 'transference' proper, by which I mean the *projecting* on to people in the present of feelings that really belong to people in the past, often, though not exclusively, parents. As such, transference is always, in *one* sense, inappropriate because feelings have become attached to the wrong person.

There is a difficult issue here for ministers and it is to do with whether we should and can accept being treated as if we were somebody else or possessed greater powers than we feel we have. Humanly and naturally we can react in either of two ways. If, for example, it *suits* something in our own personality to be treated as a strong, even perfect, parent figure we are vulnerable to accepting this role totally and uncritically whenever it is asked of us.

On the other hand if it makes us very uncomfortable to be treated in this way we can hurry to disabuse the other person of all such ideas, sometimes clumsily and without thought to the particular situation: 'I'm as human as you are: I have as many doubts about God as you do.' This *may* be an appropriate stance to take up, but in any given situation we may be acting like a doctor who on a pre-operative visit to a patient insists on talking of the dangers of the operation and his own lack of experience of it at a time when the patient *needs* to 'let go', trust and co-operate and is indeed in a vulnerable, childlike position.

The nature of ministry and pastoral care means that we *are* asked to bear being more than ourselves, to partcipate in what some would identify as the *collective archetype*[4] of priesthood and/or wisdom, and to accept, for example, a sustaining, guiding or containing role. If we can become able to carry the 'universal' hopes and fears projected on to and into us by those to whom we minister then we can enable a new and positive process to begin.

As we have seen, the hopes and fears pertaining to the religious dimension of life tend to be powerful, inaccessible, potentially uncontrollable and so quite frightening. But as they become 'incarnate' and focused in the *human being* of the minister, they can show a *human* face, become *human* size and so more manageable. Our willingness to *bear* projections is therefore the first essential in this process, and the ministry of pastoral care requires it. We cannot abrogate the sustaining role. But there is another side to the coin.

There are times when we need to assert the reality of the situation. We are human, subject to human limitations and we *will* fail to meet people's more-than-human hopes. Even as a doctor has to stand aside and allow a recovering patient to rediscover and trust their own strength so as ministers we have, at the right moment, to stand aside and allow people's faith and hope to become truly, humanly and internally theirs. The dilemma is how not to let people down *too soon* and *too abruptly,* and can only be resolved by considerable work on our own self-awareness and the nurturing of our own inner strength.

Ideally, we want to know what is happening to us at any moment, how much and in what way we are being treated as somebody we are not, and be able, sensitively, to judge how much to let it happen and when to modify it by the reality of our humanness. But that is a counsel of perfection. We have the pressure of our own unconscious upon us and we have to gain our awareness in the midst of often very complex situations. We are, for example, rightly the colleague and even the friend of the churchwarden at one moment and his or her priest or minister at another. Counsellors and psychotherapists avoid these multiple roles but for ministers to be able to function in them is of the essence of pastoral care.

The *managing* of projections is, therefore, a vital and positive part of our task as ministers to help others (and ourselves) come to know the great *realities* of our relationship with each other and with God. But as we have seen in earlier chapters the mechanism of projection often functions negatively as a reality-avoiding, reality-distorting form of defence. It is probably the most common of the primitive defences, and most, if not all of us, use it at least some of the time. In this negative form it can operate very easily between a religious body and its ministers, and I now want to explore in more detail some particular areas of potential difficulty and confusion.

We have already seen in the last chapter[5] how a minister or congregation can get into difficulties over sexuality if avoidance or projection, by either party, are involved. We are not sure what was happening in the situation that had developed between John and his female parishioners, except that he didn't like their attentions and was feeling uncomfortable about them; we are not told how *they* felt. Or we learned also of the situation between Peter and the bereaved widow in his congregation. This is potentially an explosive situation, when one person has lost someone and is lonely and cut off, and the other person is trying to offer comfort. Jane had her own reading of the situation, based no doubt on her desperate feelings about her marriage, but we are left not quite sure what was going on, and quite how Peter was involved.

The whole area of sexuality is vulnerable to the defensive use of projection. If we, either as ministers, or as members of a congregation, have avoided our sexuality or aspects of it we may *split* it off from the rest of our being, *project* it out from us and see it only in *others.* So we can be fearing, yet unconsciously wanting and even attracting some form of sexual involvement, and this conflict can result in either party misperceiving sexual desire in the other. This can happen in all walks of life, but the pastoral scene is especially vulnerable to it. Our unconscious fear makes use of the 'safety' of the pastoral role; our unconscious yet forbidden desire makes us wonder if the other person is attracted to us. So we need to work to become conscious of our *own* sexuality because only then can we begin to disentangle whose is the desire at any given point in order to prevent the escalation of an undesirable and unprofessional involvement. Otherwise this may happen and then there is a tendency to back off hurriedly leaving the other party feeling 'led on' and then let down and sometimes extremely and destructively angry about this. If humiliation has been involved then the resulting mess can have very nasty and prolonged reverberations indeed.

Another thing that can happen in this area is a confusion of projections. A parishioner may actually unconsciously be wanting a parent rather than a lover, this desire being stimulated at least partially by the imagery of the Church, which casts the minister in a parental role. The issue, for him

or her, may be dependence rather than sexuality, particularly
if the former is an area of life in which he or she has not
matured or has temporarily lost balance, as sometimes
happens in, for example, bereavement. The strong underlying
need is for a father or mother — a need unresolved from
childhood — and the adult sexuality which may *seem* to be
uppermost is being used as a way to ward off this painful
area. But we, as ministers on the receiving end of all this, are
in danger of seeing *only* sexual desire and advance,
particularly if we ourselves have unresolved needs about
either sexuality or dependence. If, because of these, we cannot
'get the right message' we will be confused and in danger of
becoming either cruelly rejecting or collusively indulgent of
the other person as a defence against confronting the issues
in ourselves.

The sorting out of these sorts of projections is something
for which theological training and rabbinical college little
prepares the newly-ordained pastor. Even when we have
been theoretically prepared it is something we tend to learn
more about from bitter experience. The gaining of this
experience can be very stressful, and at times, especially
without adequate support and help, but sometimes even with
it, it becomes a source of breakdown and scandal for all
concerned. A great part of the difficulty is that we tend to
find this area very hard to talk about, particularly, perhaps,
with other ministers for we are often beset by a strong sense
of shame.

Difficulties over projection happen, of course, in other
bodies, public and private, but in the religious world *God* can
be an additional complicating factor, in that a whole other
dimension of projection is potentially available to us. Human
ideas about parents, judges, and kings can be ascribed to
God and made total articles of faith, and then complicated by
the fact that the true and complete nature of God is
unknowable. We cannot do what is helpful and indeed
necessary in reducing purely human projections, which is to
test them against reality — for we cannot know if we have
anything like a conception of the true being of God against
which to test *our* reality. For one thing, he/she is not separate
enough from us; for it is claimed that in him/her 'we live and
move and have our being'.[6]

A further complication is that any or all of what is projected upon God can also be projected upon ministers as his representatives. So we can find ourselves invested with all love, all power, all sternness, all punitiveness. The accent here should be on the word *all*; we are given all these things without limit and often without any of the balancing influence of their other poles.

Sometimes a form of *splitting* emerges; we would, for example, really like to be angry with God, but that is unthinkable so we vent our spleen on his representative instead, that is the poor minister. This is particularly hard to bear when, in cases of tragedy or unjust suffering, the wrath and hate that are around are very intense, yet they are very hard to uncover and begin to put in their right place. This happens sometimes at times of bereavement when people's unallowed anger with God comes out on the minister for not being caring enough or not providing the 'right' comfort at the funeral service.

One way and another, congregations do sometimes tend to have very unrealistic expectations of their human ministers; they must have unlimited time and availability and indefatigable good humour. They must even be prepared to act as a whipping boy for God himself if need be. The individual or corporate anger with ministers who cannot or choose not to fulfil these expectations can be extreme. Their misdemeanours are seen as more serious; they are not 'allowed' to fail, have moral lapses or a broken marriage. Sometimes they are not 'allowed' to be as they are, and here the attack can be vicious, as the controversies over homosexual ministers show.

It is very difficult for those of us in ministry to withstand the strength of such projections and attacks, wherever they come from, particularly if they chime in with something in our own unconscious such as an overriding need to be loved and found lovable. Furthermore, I have also already indicated that there is a degree of projection that we rightly need to contain and carry; thus we do not have an unlimited licence to violate people's expectations of us.

However, there is a difference between this and the honest realization that, even when we try to be sensitive, we cannot be all things to all men. If we are always trying to push away our real limitations the resulting sense of strain and stress can be tremendous. Unfortunately the build-up of this sort of strain is hard to recognize; it may suit both ministers and people and ministers and other ministers to leave it this way, and so remain undetected for a long time. Becoming aware is also painful but in the long term facilitates a greater personal and corporate freedom.

Ministers' family lives

I want to end this chapter with a short section focusing on the situation — or plight, we might say — of ministers' families in relation to some of the processes we have looked at. This exercise is justified, even though not all ministers have, or are allowed to have, spouses and families because a large proportion do have and many of them are put under strain.

The first thing we have to note is that the entity of 'minister's family' has changed shape rather dramatically in recent times. Up to a relatively short while ago we could have assumed that they were made up of ministers, wives and children. Now we have female rabbis, female Free Church ministers and female deacons; for all of these, their husbands may or may not be in the same line of business. This puts a whole new complexion on the external situation but many of the underlying issues are unchanged. These concern people's motives, half conscious and half unconscious, for marrying a minister: often to do with *idealizing* them and so being vulnerable to great disillusion when the ideal turns out to have feet of clay. If and when this happens isolation is a further hazard, for clergy and their spouses often feel they cannot turn to anyone when their marriage is in difficulties.

Of our five case histories the story of Peter and Jane best exemplifies the general situation. We have some sense that Robert's relationship with his wife is not always smooth, but also that it might have been this way whatever profession or career Robert had adopted. For Peter and Jane and their family things seem to be different; it is clear that some of their problems have arisen just because Peter is a minister.

We need to look at their and other people's situations in terms of the 'two stories' we have been exploring in this chapter. First, the 'top level' story of what is relatively easily observable, and second, the more hidden 'underneath' story.

According to the 'top' story Peter and Jane have a lot in common with other working couples. There has been some conflict over Jane working at all, and now she is doing so their working hours do not coincide. Peter, being a minister, tends to work evenings and of course Sundays and parts of Saturday; Jane does nursing shifts. So they are going to have trouble getting time together, and it will be hard not to get into a 'notes left on the fridge' situation. Not an ideal system at any time, it is severely under strain during their present difficult time with their son. Indeed the latter's behaviour may, in part, be a protest against this very system.

Another issue that is common to ministers' marriages and those of others who work with people is that of confidentiality and its limits. How much can work problems be shared with the other partner without breaching confidentiality? This issue is complicated by the fact that whatever the couple decide this may not coincide with the perceptions of those outside. 'Will he or she *really* not tell his or her other half what I said when I came for help or just a chat yesterday?' goes the thought. Yet often this doubt is not made explicit and dealt with, but lingers on promoting difficult areas of distrust.

Nor does the distrust come only from one side. We saw how Jane was very suspicious of the sort of relationship Peter was having with his bereaved parishioner, quite apart from her resentment that it was taking up a lot of his time at very unsocial hours. The difficulty is that there is no easy way for her to allay her fears, and probably no way she can ease them by sharing them with anyone else. At the moment her usual trust in her husband has gone because of their other difficulties, yet she has nothing else to fall back on as a way out of this dilemma.

This sort of difficulty is not peculiar to ministers' families, but it is made worse for them because such a family has to live as if it was in a bubble encapsulated by its community and watched intently by it. The problems become horribly public, and the task of the family too complex. For most families this task is twofold; in addition to the maintenance of family life they have to prepare their members to meet and participate in the outside world, to take jobs and to contribute as members of the community. Ministers' families have additionally to represent and exemplify the religious tradition for those to whom they minister.

At this point we begin to enter into the interplay between the 'top' and 'bottom'[7] stories of their life. All the processes we described earlier in the chapter begin to impinge upon the family. We know Jane is complaining that Peter is married to everything but her. Perhaps Peter is succumbing to the pressures demanding total availability. It might of course be even worse if Jane shared this outlook and was not an independent working wife; the myth might become even more intense and entrenched. And at least the fact that they are quarrelling about it may bring it to light and stop intolerable overwork and strain building up.

Then, of course, there is the pressure to be good and even perfect as a model of family life. Their son Jonathan is already exploding this by his behaviour, but in the short term the consequences of this for Peter and Jane are exceedingly unpleasant. It has raised their anxiety level to a point where they fear the worst, not without some justification. This hardly provides any sort of suitable climate for sorting out the difficulties they are having with their son. Jonathan is a thorn in the flesh to them at present, and is not likely to receive the most sympathetic understanding: to them he is letting the side down and letting the unthinkable happen; he is proclaiming to the world that the minister's family has feet of clay.

More hidden still are the sort of rivalries and jealousies that the very fact of Peter being married can engender. Again these can come from both directions. On the one hand there may well be quite strong but unacknowledged resentment and jealousy among some of the congregation that somebody has Peter all to herself, even if this is manifestly not the case. This may result in strong but often quite heavily disguised attacks on the family unit. Peter and Jane are perhaps picking up something of this when they wonder whether people would be supportive or destructive if their marriage really did go on the rocks. In many ways it is a fair question. On the other hand what of Jane's feelings about having to share her husband with so many others, who may want and be able to talk to him of more intimate things than she can manage, especially at the moment when they feel so estranged from each other? It's more than galling to contemplate that others may be achieving what she cannot. This problem of course is particularly bad at present, but I think it always lurks somewhere in these sorts of situations.

Lastly, we come to the difficult-to-describe area where some of the projections that go on between a minister and his congregation can also operate within the family unit itself. What does it mean emotionally for Jane to have the representative of God as a husband or Jonathan to have him as a father? We gather that Jonathan is, to an extent, in touch with this difficulty in his outcry 'How would you like to have a minister for a father?', but he probably cannot make real or complete sense of it. I do not think we pay enough attention to the complications on a deep level of relating to someone in the family set-up at one moment and at the altar the next. It is possible that sometimes the human dimension gets obscured, making ordinary family relationships and perhaps particularly a couple's sexual relationship subject to strange distortion and more than a hint of unreality. We know that Peter and Jane are finding that their sexual life is not going very well; we do not know what has caused this or even if it is something that has been present at a lower level from before the onset of their present bad patch.

Furthermore, it is also often true that what a ministerial couple find most hard to share and communicate is their experience of God and the spiritual dimension. We think it should be easy and then find that somehow it is very hard, because there are too many defences operating. Either or both may *deny* doubt and difficulty in prayer; there may be rivalry as to who has got furthest along the spiritual path, showing in one being put down by the other, or holiness and humanness may be *split* and located exclusively in one or other of the couple.

Peter and Jane are just one couple, but their story could be multiplied. I have not attempted to 'sort them out', but rather to lay bare the sorts of pressure that they could be struggling with. Their position is, I think, more complicated than that of other 'normal' couples and families, just because of the possible depth and breadth not only of their feelings, but also of the community around them.

In more general conclusion to this chapter I think and hope we may have had a glimpse of how powerful feelings are; they are, moreover, inevitable and vital to our whole life. But without understanding and reflection they can seem out of control and become merely a source of worry and disturbance. What I have tried to do, in struggling to describe some of the processes I believe to be going on, is to name something of what may feel unmentionable in the hope that this will be a way to contain and lower anxiety and strain.

Notes

1. See ch. 3, pp. 64—6 and ch. 6, pp. 105—6, 109, 110.
2. 14 April 1987.
3. See ch. 8, pp. 158—62.
4. *Collective archetype*: the name given to a word, idea or fantasy which is felt to have a universal, partly unconscious power or emotional significance in relation to our collective experience. The archetypal idea itself is universal across cultures, though the form in which it is 'filled out' and expressed varies across cultures.

   Here I am following the thought of C. G. Jung. For a summary see: A. Storr *Jung*, Fontana 1973, ch. 3.
5. See ch. 8, pp. 163—6.
6. Acts 17.28.
7. *'Top' and 'bottom' stories*; as in myth. See pp. 172—4.

TEN

What to do about it

The foregoing chapters have attempted to describe and explore some of the more hidden sources of strain and stress for those in ministry. It remains to think a little more about how they can be withstood and dealt with, preferably before they get out of hand. Ministry *is* stressful, and the management of potential stress is properly part of growth and development. Breakdown does sometimes happen and need not be disastrous for it can be a starting point for something better; indeed for some people it may have to happen if they are going to change and mature. But a gradual growth, when possible, is obviously more desirable.

The most important thing needed is the availability of support *and* the ability to make use of it. The latter is not as easy as it sounds for the first hurdle is the acceptance that we in the helping professions need help and support for ourselves. This is amply illustrated in Robert's story. But from where can support come? From family and friends? Yes, surely, where this is possible. But some ministers live alone as John and, we surmise, Elizabeth do, and for them the principle of confidentiality prevents them being as open about some of their difficulties as they might really want to be. And it is clear from Peter and Jane's story, and from the last chapter, that ministers' marriages quite often get sucked in and become part of the problem instead of being part of the support system.

Does support come from bishops, religious superiors or the hierarchy? Yes, again in so far as the general attitude of those in authority makes life more or less smooth for those accountable to them. But there are difficulties here. We saw how Anne was quite sure that her Superior would not understand. To Robert, the supportive attempts of his bishop were more a source of trial than a support, and Elizabeth's efforts to get support from her boss ended in failure, because he, probably rightly, felt he could not mix the roles of counsellor and boss. This is a particular instance of a more general problem. In the Church of England, for example, a minister's bishop is at one and the same time his father-in-God *and* the representative of the institution which employs him. It is not easy to mix what are essentially the two different functions of personal support and line management. It is my impression that the religious bodies have been rather reluctant to recognize this difficulty, perhaps believing that it will, somehow, be all right because the institutions are supposed to be caring and high-principled, and not realizing that these are not the issues here. Be that as it may, it is clear that some ministers would rather not let their religious superiors know when they are in difficulties just because they fear the implications this could have for their career and indeed their whole future.

There are some dioceses in the Church of England and the Roman Catholic Church which *have* pinpointed this difficulty and provided systems of support and accountability which try to address the issue of the need for confidential consultancy.[1] But implementing this is bound to be more difficult when the impetus has come 'from the top', and operates within the usual boundaries of the system. There will be questions like 'how much can we say?' or 'is it personal or professional support, and where do we draw the line?'. That there are such questions does not mean that the system cannot work, but these questions and difficulties need to be made and kept *conscious,* and faced, rather than being allowed to rumble on in the background or the depths.

One of the reasons why any system of support that involves the hierarchy may fail is that the depth of the problem is not being addressed. The 'top' story identifies only the role conflict between support and accountability. The 'underneath' story goes farther than this.

Because as ministers we can *project* father images on to bishops and other leaders we are vulnerable to the emergence of the dynamic of 'caring bishop/father and frightened minister/child'. Robert is caught in something of this. His bishop is trying to be caring; he is defending against this by irritation and rejection of the attempt, but he may well be defending also against a *fear* in himself. Is *this* father really benign or not?

Unless this second story is faced and understood, practical initiatives in the 'top level' story will not work.

Other dioceses and bodies have provided the possibility of *peer* support from an early stage in ministry, most often in groups.[2] They are making the point, often building on some aspects of, for example, theological college life, that *sharing* can be an integral and natural part of ministry. But being personally open in a group can seem rather threatening, for peer pressure sometimes feels even worse than that of authority.

One of the best systems may therefore be one where the group is not sponsored or arranged by the hierarchy, but is facilitated by an outside conductor who, amongst other things, will *see fair play* in the peer group milieu. Unfortunately it is still a minority of ministers who feel able to avail themselves of the opportunity. Those who do so are often those who are most open and aware to start with.

The more traditional, and probably more generally acceptable, disciplines of self-evaluation through spiritual direction, confession and retreat continue to be available. These do afford complete confidentiality but cannot offer peer support as a regular built-in factor in everyday working life.

Some ministers, and those five who have accompanied us through this book are probably among them, come to feel the need for more specialist and focused help for the difficulties they are experiencing, particularly but not exclusively, if the difficulties have gone so far as to give rise to physical or emotional symptoms. Before, though, we look in detail at the kinds of help that can be made available, there is to my mind a prior question and it is this: '*Who* actually needs the help?', or put in another way, 'Where can we best intervene so as to produce the greatest and most lasting relief of strain?'.

We can concentrate on the *individual,* as indeed probably should be the case with John and Elizabeth. The story of Peter and Jane raises options. Is it Peter who really needs the help, Jane, or their son? Do they need help on an individual level, or would it be best if they could consider themselves as a *couple* or even a family unit? With Anne and Robert we could take the issues wider still. Is there something in the *systems* of religious communities or the Church of England which means that things can go awry very easily? I am not here suggesting that we should neglect the distress of the individual — far from it — but unless we also approach the stresses hidden in the systems and institutions in some way then difficulties with individual people are likely to recur.

A word of warning is needed here. There has been, in the name of psychological awareness, some desire to make religious communities and church congregations function too much like encounter or sensitivity groups, intent on exploring their own processes *all the time*. Under this pattern some individuals crack, and the whole atmosphere becomes too electric and anxiety-laden for any unselfconscious rhythm of functioning.

In any case the extent to which we can focus on the wider bodies depends on the availability of resources, and these tend to be scanty. A necessary prerequisite to the providing of more resources is the recognition of the problem, particularly those aspects of it which tend to be more unconscious and hidden from us. We cannot instantly provide resources, but we can continue to work on greater consciousness.

Let us now return to exploring what help we can offer to an individual. It seems to me that this is of three kinds. First, and we cannot neglect this, severe physical symptoms are going, in the first instance, to need physical and probably medical help. This becomes a necessity even if it is also thought that the symptoms either have an emotional origin, or that emotional factors are making a considerable contribution to their maintenance. Some relief from pain, infection or irritation is required if the person is to continue to be able to function at work and at home. We see this in John's story. We have already surmised that emotional factors, both past and present, are playing a large part in the reappearance of his ulcer at this time. But the fact remains, that he *has* got an ulcer, and in the immediate short term he probably *is* going to need medical help. We could say that at least initially he has taken himself to the right place in going to the doctor.

The point, though, is that help may well stay on the level of the relief of symptoms and be essentially palliative, rather than genuinely healing unless the more underlying and hidden causes can also be looked at. After all we know that this is at least the second time in his life that John has been afflicted in this way. What could happen is that he could get better from this physical ailment, become vulnerable to others and never really feel well. It could also mean that he might undergo ever more extensive medical investigations and even operations unless his more total being receives attention.

As with general medical intervention so also with intervention aimed more directly but still medically at the relief of emotional states. If a depression such as Anne's deepens, or panic anxiety such as Elizabeth's is maintained so that everyday functioning becomes severely impeded and breakdown threatens, then we may have to enlist the help of the psychiatric services and even admission to hospital can be indicated. All this is a difficult area; it is still regarded as very stigmatizing, and unexplained gaps in c.v.s can be prejudicial to people's futures. Part of the reason for this may well be that it is an area of which we are *all* internally, and perhaps unconsciously, deeply afraid and want to push it away from us.

Something of this dilemma can sometimes be avoided by using private psychiatric and psychological help, but in the case of the latter, particularly, the problem then often becomes economic, for psychotherapy can take a long time. Indeed ministers and ministerial families in some geographical areas may, by reason of their relatively low income level, have no alternative but to use the, often limited, help that is made available on the NHS. In regions better served by counselling services or in dioceses where there *does* exist a referral network and somebody to co-ordinate it this aspect of the problem is somewhat eased.

What we need to do overall is to promote a form of *education* whereby the need to have recourse to help for our emotions is not seen as something awful, invariably implying that the person is vulnerable for life and a risky employment or preferment bet. This problem is not confined to the religious world — as I said above, we all fear this dimension — but the Church and other religious bodies do not have a particularly good track record in this area. Rather cruel defences get used against emotional problems such as insinuations of moral weakness or spiritual incapacity.

There are, too, more insidious difficulties stemming from the 'underneath' story of ministry, lay as well as ordained. First, we often have, as helpers, a resistance to being helped ourselves, for the acceptance of the need makes a hole in our human 'shield' and our fantasized omnipotence, this last backed up by a mistaken perception of the relationship between our ministry and that of God. Second, on the 'giving' level we are exposed to the danger of overusing our avowed *caring* capacities to the point of making the unfortunate recipient feel just a patient and the *object* of care; this can make the recovery of self-respect extremely difficult.

Furthermore, I think it is possible that Christianity, in particular, may have a strangely impeding role in recovery from *depression.* The genesis of depression often lies in some level of *anger* that has been *denied* or has not been able to be expressed. We have seen that anger is not an easy emotion for Christianity, and the faith itself may actually get in the way of recovery. A complicating factor is that those suffering from depression often seem, on the surface, to be particularly 'nice' people, nice Christians, nice ministers. The fact that not-so-nice things are smouldering away underneath is not recognized. It is easy then for a sense of global helplessness — 'this is how I am, this is how it is inevitably going to be, and I can't do anything about it' — to set in and become like an enveloping sodden wet blanket. Unfortunately this 'blanket' gets shared and even extended by other like-minded people under the guise of mutual sympathy and compassion. The intention is sincere and good, and I am not disputing that, but the whole can degenerate into a process of mutual identification and fusion in which the depression actually deepens. This can happen whether it is a member of the congregation *or* the minister who is originally afflicted.

This said, it is important to acknowledge that there are few states of mind capable of causing more suffering to a human being than severe depression. It is also an over-simplification to presume that unacknowledged anger is *always* at the bottom of it, but in so far as anger and non-niceness *are* implicated, the religious bodies, more than some others, may not be able to be of the maximum help and support.

What sometimes also happens is that depression gets relabelled as the 'dark night of the soul' of St John of the Cross.[3] It is very difficult to distinguish this, or that which comes under the heading of Thomas Merton's existential 'dread'[4], from the sort of depression that could and should be alleviated. Probably we cannot always make this distinction, for psychological and spiritual do overlap, but perhaps we can learn to pause a moment before we presume their total identity.

We turn now to the other two sources of help that can be found for a minister suffering stress and discomfort. They are both psychological but divide broadly along the lines of first, *anxiety management/self-help* and second, some form of *counselling* or *psychotherapy*. In the latter a particular form of relationship is offered as the main ingredient; in the former the emphasis is on the individual *learning* better ways of coping.

Anxiety management/self-help

Under the heading of self-help come some of the elements we have already looked at in these pages; they come to have a preventative, rather than only curative, function. They can be subsumed under the heading of our taking responsibility for our own health. Time off, hobbies, safeguarding of time with family and non-work friends and participation in the refreshment and stimulation of in-service training are all part of this.

In short, we have to learn to love and take care of ourselves. Often it is the acceptance of this *principle* that is the most difficult first step; after this the '*how to do it*' becomes relatively obvious.

Apart from this general principle, ministry *is* stressful and the knowledge of tried and even technical ways of managing anxiety may be extremely helpful to some people. I am speaking here of such practices as muscular relaxation, and the learning of particular ways of thinking in anxiety-laden situations so that their impact on the person lessens. Sometimes it is most helpful to experience these with other people in a group since this gives the added support of reducing isolation through sharing concerns and difficulties.

Muscular relaxation involves, in its most fundamental form, taking time — probably twenty minutes to half an hour — to relax the whole body. Paradoxically, to do this we need first to tense the body and then let go, to the accompaniment of breathing in and out. Often it is easiest to regulate the process by a system of counting for tensing and relaxing. The idea is to choose a comfortable position and go through the body in small 'chunks' starting, for example, from the fingers of the hand, moving up the arm, and then to the legs, head, torso, etc. This is the core of the process and usually involves an initial period of regular and extended practice. But we cannot always go off and lie down in the middle of an anxiety-provoking situation! So we need to be able to modify and extend the technique so that we can carry out its essential form unobtrusively.

This means of coping with anxiety is mainly on the autonomic physiological level, and for most people it is not enough. Our bodies, often going too 'fast' in anxiety, are additionally or even causally stimulated by our thoughts, feelings and even our actual behaviour. We can illustrate this last point by Elizabeth, who was beginning to have attacks of panic whilst out shopping. The most natural reaction in the world after such an unpleasant experience as hers — for panic attacks *are* extremely unpleasant, often producing sensations of being unable to breathe, faintness or fear of dying — is to try to *avoid* having the experience again, usually by avoiding the activity during which it happened. Unfortunately this is also the most unhelpful and disastrous behaviour to adopt because to the fear of the actual situation is added the fear of the fear which is kept at bay, yet *maintained* by the avoidance. Avoidance precludes any testing of the reality, and is only too likely to spread to other activities and situations. It is the reverse of the old principle, which has a lot of sense in it — having fallen off a horse, get back on it quick! But I would want to modify this with some gentleness: get back on the horse, but choose a quiet horse or a quiet back street for the next outing!

Similarly, progression back from the path of phobic avoidance has to be slow, needing to start with occasions that are not too difficult — the corner shop rather than the supermarket — and accepting some relapses as inevitable, but trying not to be deflected from the overall way of non-avoidance. This is hard but, particularly when anxiety is affecting the most ordinary of life processes, it has to be done lest we compound our difficulties with isolation. It is much more difficult to do than to write about, and if fear has really gained a grip on us we sometimes need, for a while, the sympathetic, but not too protective, help of another person.

Management of anxiety cannot, however, be completed by our dealing only with our physiology or our behaviour. For human beings think and feel as well as sense and act; indeed we need to think to begin to make an essentially human, controllable sense of our anxiety when in its essence it seems so unpredictable and uncontrolled. So relaxation can be combined with imagination of pleasant restful scenes, or indeed even with images of the anxiety-producing scene, which may then lose some of its power in combination or competition with the relaxation technique.

More important, perhaps, is a sort of *self-talk* in anxiety situations. For example we can ask ourselves: What is the worst that could happen? Is it likely to happen — Yes/No? If 'no' then perhaps I don't need to keep on thinking about it; if 'Yes', will it be really disastrous, and if it happens what could I actually do about it?

Another need is for the acceptance of some fear and anxiety in ourselves. If we are anxiety-*less* then we are also likely to be dead! We can ask ourselves: Would it be human and healthy to feel no anxiety in this situation (the answer is probably, 'No'), or: Is my anxiety inevitably going to escalate out of all proportion?, or: Does it matter if I don't get 100 per cent relief; do I have to be a perfect human being?; answers, again, probably 'No'.

These are examples of the kind of self-talk we can use. There is quite a considerable body of research and literature on this area which I cannot reproduce here, though the chapter notes point to it.[5] The point is that there are quite a lot of everyday ways of coping with stress and anxiety that we can make available to ourselves. On the whole these approaches are designed to deal with the 'here and now' of our strain and anxiety experiences. They do not try to probe our underlying feelings, or look for their causes in either our present or past history. It is my impression that they work best when the strain has not become very established or very acute, and as such they can be a useful 'hygiene' for all of us in our everyday lives.

An element of choice also comes in. Some people, and they tend to be those with firmer defence systems, *prefer* to deal with themselves on the level of learning to regulate their own responses; others are more interested in their *feelings* about things and *curious* about what may underlie their fears and problems. If we are such people we feel, intuitively, that our current difficulty is part of a wider aspect of ourselves; we may realize that it stems from conflicts that have been around a long time and that represent more fundamental dimensions of our being. We are then more likely to seek, for our healing and growth, some form of counselling or psychotherapy, either individually or in a group. These processes aim to acknowledge and explore thoughts and feelings, even those we have *repressed* or *denied.* But before we consider them in more detail I want to return to the notion of *choice.*

To face and explore unknown parts of ourselves is an enterprise not lightly to be embarked upon. The potential *gains* are great: a more solid basis in ourselves for living, more of ourselves available to live and more vital energy with which to live. In other words, a greater fundamental *freedom.* But the enterprise demands commitment, a willingness and some ability to tolerate the emergence of painful feelings, and for many of us it will mean that we have to face and work through some *regret* and *mourning* that are the price of awareness: regret over past choices, now seen to be precipitate or immature, mourning over lost opportunities that cannot come again.

Over the last years, when working with many different sorts of people from a wide variety of backgrounds, I have come to temper my initial therapeutic enthusiasm with experience. I have come to know that people's own sense in this area needs to be respected, lest an attempt at psychotherapeutic exploration leaves them in a worse state than before. They can become stuck in a different way, in the pain of some of the feelings they were previously defending against without being able to make the necessary internal resolution of them. Others can embark on a counselling process, be unable to lower their high defences and end up frustrated and disillusioned. Worse still, if they should be in positions of influence they are likely to try to dissuade others who in all probability could use this sort of help. Yet others still would not dream of entering such a process: in the case of those within the religious dimension the *rationalization* for not doing so is often that it will 'destroy' their faith.

We have, therefore, a *dilemma*. We have seen, in these pages, something of the real harm ministers who are unaware can do to themselves and those to whom they minister; the potential for this is heightened because of the primitive raw material of the religious dimension and the representative, leadership function of ministry. For the health of the religious bodies it is vitally important that as ministers we should be aware. Yet we cannot push some people beyond their personal limits.

The key to this dilemma must, at least partially, lie in the process of *selection* and *training*. We need to take more account, in selection, of the criterion of personal *emotional* suitability for the work of ministry, without an over-reliance on the dimensions of the 'grace of the office' having to make up for our human deficits over/against the very difficult area of a person's own subjective sense of vocation. This will inevitably mean saying 'no' to some people and facing all the difficulties associated with making this judgement objectively, and the anger and pain that, in the short term, it inevitably causes.

I am not, in this, advocating trying to select *perfect* ministers; that would be to fall into precisely some of the traps we have identified. It is more about whether and how we can select people who will be 'good enough'; human people with human failings but people who, given support, will be able to grow and develop into their vocation and role.

Of course we shall not get this process quite right and it would not necessarily be a good thing if we could; it might encourage in us a smug complacency. But we need to encourage people to develop as far as they are able, and to pay more attention to suiting people to particular posts and particular aspects of ministry. It is here that in-service training or continuing ministerial education, as it is now called, is not optional but vital.

Counselling and psychotherapy

Both of these usually involve experiencing some of our deeper, hidden feelings and internal conflicts. Let me introduce them by returning to Robert's story.

Robert's attitude is one of being unable to trust the concern of his superiors for his well-being. We can ask how much of this stems from his childhood experience of being unaccustomed to people, notably his parents, being benignly concerned with his interests and worries. Whether his perceptions are in accordance with historical fact is neither here nor there. For the difficulty lies in the way our *internal* images from the past live on, independently of their origin, and obtrude into and colour our present-day encounters. We then use defences, as Robert did his withdrawal, to protect us from internal anxieties, but we use them when we do not really need them because we are not, in *present* reality, as vulnerable as we were in childhood. Our defences inhibit us in our present situation, and we can become impoverished as people, as Robert has, with whole parts of us pushed down and not available to us for use and development.

Psychodynamic counselling and analytical psychotherapy attempt, in essence, to trace the emergence and development of this sort of situation in the story of our earlier, childhood experience. It is then possible to 'put some things back in their right place', and so become more free in the present and future.

The difference between psychodynamically-orientated counselling and psychotherapy is notoriously difficult to pinpoint and define. The whole is complicated by the use of labels, which may bear more relationship to the setting and the traditions of training institutions than to differences in what actually goes on. This said, they probably should be seen as lying on a spectrum, with psychotherapy being *likely* to take longer than counselling. The difference between them lies in the amount of unconscious material that can be worked with, and probably the *degree,* though not the fact, of the emphasis on exploring what is going on in the developing relationship between client and counsellor or therapist.

There is only limited provision for this sort of help within the NHS, but there are agencies[6] that set out to provide it at a cost that is related to people's ability to pay. The difficulty is that many of these agencies are clustered in and around London, and it can be hard to find a counsellor or therapist within one's means if living and working in more out of the way places, but networks for finding such resources do exist.[7]

If we do seek this sort of help it does not necessarily involve a lengthy frequent analysis, intended to uncover all that has gone on in previous life. Admittedly I have indicated that some difficulties originate in quite early, obscure and difficult-to-reach childhood experiences, but I do not want to give the impression that only *very* intensive and lengthy therapy can do anything to help. The goals in shorter-term therapy need to be more limited, but much depends on our motivation to work on ourselves, as well as, obviously, upon the skill of the therapist. Both client and therapist normally try to make a responsible and realistic assessment of both the external and internal possibilities, though the person in the role of therapist inevitably brings to this process an experience which initially the client does not have.

I have not sought here to give an extensive account of counselling and psychotherapy, and have unavoidably oversimplified the issues. The chapter notes give pointers for taking the subject further.[8] I have wanted, rather, to set this kind of help within the overall context of this book.

In summary: sharing, support, counselling and psychotherapy share an aim, even if they approach it rather differently. This is to facilitate a self-awareness and an increased inner strength that will allow and encourage us to take care of ourselves, not just others, and to become reasonably good parents to ourselves whatever may have been our actual experience of childhood and growing up.

Growing self-awareness also helps us to deal with the feelings that other people inappropriately *transfer* on to and into us. We can come to recognize when they do not fit the real situation, and so not become inordinately disturbed by them. So if, as ministers, we are seen as perfect and the source of all wisdom, love and strength, growth in awareness can be a terrific relief. We realize that we cannot provide all these things, *and* that we do not have to struggle to do so. Awareness can also be salutary as we realize that it is perhaps not our unique and marvellous gifts that are drawing people to us, but rather that we are being *seen* in a particular way.

Similarly, if we can see inappropriate feelings of ingratitude, anger and attachment more clearly for what they are then the heat goes out of the situation, and we are less likely to retaliate by withdrawing or becoming rejecting and even vicious. We come to be more comfortable in the pastoral role and less strained and stressed by it.

The process is, of course, much easier to talk about than to work through in practice. It will take us a lifetime; indeed in one sense it can never be 'finished'. But psychotherapy and support schemes can help to give us some internal 'tools' to start and carry on the process, adjusting to new life events as they happen, and sometimes needing some more help if something particularly unexpected or traumatic happens.

Whatever the help that is sought and found, it is the step of beginning to recognize what may be going on that is the most basic and the most difficult. Difficult because the very extent and intensity of our involvement militates against our being able to be reflective and take a long objective look at ourselves and our situations. We have only to read again the stories of our five case histories to appreciate just how involved the issues can get. A necessary corollary of this is that I cannot claim such objectivity for myself and my writing in these pages, for I too am involved. What I hope is that my attempt to externalize my thoughts on paper can provide a provisional map of the terrain.

Notes

1. *Consultancy*: a regular, systematic review of ministry in relation to goals attained, the identification of the next steps, the overall balance of professional and personal life and career development. It is contractually undertaken, usually on an individual basis and the contract is periodically reviewed.
2. These differ from consultancy in that they provide an opportunity for regular sharing in a *group,* and as such offer a breadth of possibilities for feedback, support and confrontation. In such groups the level of interaction and the degree of personal and professional self-disclosure varies and is negotiated either explicitly or implicitly in the group interaction.

3. The 'dark night of the soul' is a state of subjectively experienced darkness and confusion often extending both to 'everyday' emotional life and the life of prayer. See E. Allison Peers trs., ed. *The Complete Works of St John of the Cross* Burns and Oates 1951, vol. 1, *The Dark Night of the Soul*.

4. Thomas Merton *Contemplative Prayer*, Darton, Longman and Todd 1973, esp. chs 16, 18.

5. e.g. Tom Cox *Stress*, Macmillan 1978, 'Preface'; D. Meichenbaum *Coping with Stress*, Century Publishing 1983; D. Rowe *Depression: the Way Out of Your Prison*, Routledge and Kegan Paul 1983.

6. Such as the Westminster Pastoral Foundation national network or the Dympna Centre in London. The latter restricts its work to the care of clergy and Religious.

7. Such as the Westminster Pastoral Foundation's network of Affiliated Centres; and Diocesan Advisers on Pastoral Care and Counselling, where these exist (inquiries to Diocesan Offices).

   Information about the network of the Association for Pastoral Care and Counselling, the various psychotherapy organizations and counsellors available in specific areas can be obtained from The British Association for Counselling, 37a Sheep Street, Rugby, Warwickshire.

8. For example, M. Jacobs *Still Small Voice: An Introduction to Counselling.* SPCK 1982; and J. Dominian *Make or Break: An Introduction to Marriage Counselling.* SPCK 1984, both in the New Library of Pastoral Care series.

   For a description of various models of counselling see B. Proctor *Counselling Shop*, Burnett Books with Andre Deutsch 1978; D. Brown and J. Pedder *Introduction to Psychotherapy*, Tavistock Publications 1979; or A. Storr *The Art of Psychotherapy*, Secker and Warburg and William Heinemann 1979.

Index

207